JACQUELINE KENNEDY

Here is a revealing biography of the remarkable woman who made a great impact on America; who graced the White House with beauty and charm; who won the admiration of the world with her example of heroic dignity.

Detailed with photographs, anecdotes, and much personal information never before published, this is the story of Jacqueline Bouvier Kennedy's childhood, her school days, her debut, her career as an inquiring photographer for the *Washington Times-Herald,* her marriage, her life as wife and mother, and as homemaker and one of the greatest First Ladies of all time.

Gordon Langley Hall and Ann Pinchot also touch upon Mrs. Kennedy's life today and look, with insight and understanding, on her role and influence on the heritage of America.

"The latest publication, and probably the best, about Jacqueline Kennedy . . . the story of a life that produced a woman who remained calm and poised in an hour so tragic to the nation and herself."

—Houston Chronicle

JACQUELINE KENNEDY:
A Biography

Gordon Langley Hall
and Ann Pinchot

A SIGNET BOOK

Published by The New American Library

*Published as a SIGNET BOOK
by arrangement with Frederick Fell, Inc.,
who have authorized this softcover edition.
A hardcover edition is available from Frederick Fell, Inc.*

FIRST PRINTING, JANUARY, 1966

Picture editorship, Nancy Clare Fell

SIGNET TRADEMARK REG. U.S. PAT. OFF. AND FOREIGN COUNTRIES
REGISTERED TRADEMARK—MARCA REGISTRADA
HECHO EN CHICAGO, U.S.A.

*SIGNET BOOKS are published by
The New American Library, Inc.
1301 Avenue of the Americas, New York, New York 10019*

PRINTED IN THE UNITED STATES OF AMERICA

Illustrations

(Illustrations will be found between pp. 96–99)

The Kennedy family together at St. Stephen the Martyr Roman Catholic Church in Middleburg, Virginia

The President slumped down in the car just after the rifle shot. Jacqueline leaned over him as an unidentified man lends assistance.

Jacqueline Kennedy and family attend the President's funeral

Jacqueline Kennedy walks to her husband's grave

On a visit to Arlington National Cemetery

Jacqueline and Robert F. Kennedy, with a model from the J.F.K. exhibit which will tour the United States

JACQUELINE KENNEDY

A BIOGRAPHY

She was never an ordinary woman, and on a day in November, 1963, in Dallas, Texas, she became an extraordinary one.

Jacqueline Bouvier Kennedy had found her place in history.

Her magnificent sense of dignity during the days of crisis that followed her husband's assassination helped, more than anything else, to restore an atmosphere of sanity to a shocked nation. The woman whose role in the White House had originally been likened to that of the glittering Dolley Madison, now found herself cast as the tragic Mary Todd Lincoln.

Her courage and her innate sense of fitness as to what was correct in the final national farewell to her martyred husband, were applauded not only in her native land but throughout the world. Hearts of young and old were moved by the sight of the valiant young woman and her two small children walking behind her husband's flag-draped casket.

This was a young woman who only twenty-four hours previously had been admired, envied, emulated and sometimes criticized. As a child, she had been independent, obstinate, merry and mischievous. In her background was the tradition of an old French family that had intermarried with sturdy American stock. She was named the Debutante of the Year, an honor conferred on her by the most important society reporter of the *Times*. Yet she confided to her dressmaker her fear that no one would want to marry her.

This was the girl who preferred her animals to the company of young men of her own age and often spent an evening during a dinner or ball discussing her pets, to the boredom and discomfiture of her date. This was the girl who had learned, through pain and necessity, to tune out whatever hurt or bored her, as a result of which her friends have said, "Sometimes you have the feeling she isn't really there."

This is also the mischief maker at the private school, the

good student at Vassar, the radiant bride who went blithely into marriage but with an awareness of the shoals ahead.

This was a girl who had been conditioned to the fashionable horsey life of Southampton and Aiken, with a future as a rich sophisticated member of the jet set. Yet fate sent her into the arms of a young leader whose passionate quest for peace was to influence the political climate of the entire globe. She was to become his equal partner, herself a symbol of the new generation of women, who were not only wives and mothers, but friends and partners with their husbands. She was to demonstrate that in order for a woman to fulfill her destiny to her husband and family, she must first become a true individual in her own right.

As she followed her slain young husband's body to its final resting place, was it possible that through the numbness and shock she knew with certainty that in the last years they had at last reached the peak of their own long search, that finally they could bestow generously and unselfishly upon each other the rich, nourishing rewards of a true love? That as their legend grew, it nevertheless remained rooted in reality, and that the grandeur of a rich and enduring relationship was finally theirs. And that when a sniper's bullet struck the brain of her husband, who was also John Kennedy, the thirty-fifth President of the United States, it left behind a half of the world's most remarkable partnership, a woman who would never betray her husband's trust.

The President had once said of his Jacqueline, "My wife is a very strong woman. . . ."

She proved it that day in Dallas.

Chapter One

"From the records of a nightmarish day, history will record that a woman witnessed the swearing in of the thirty-sixth President of the United States with the front of her skirt and her stockings smeared with blood.

"The woman was Mrs. John F. Kennedy. The blood was her late husband's, the thirty-fifth President of the United States."

The *News and Courier,*
Charleston, S.C.
November 23, 1963.

The President and the First Lady had taken the death of their infant son, Patrick Bouvier Kennedy, very hard.

The baby was born prematurely by Caesarian section. His death from heart failure, as the result of a lung insufficiency about thirty-nine hours and twelve minutes after his birth, was a shock the American public shared with the Kennedys. Indeed, the nation suffered vicariously and with the most profound sympathy when it heard that it was the President's sad task to tell his wife about the child's illness and death.

When Mrs. Kennedy was discharged, the sight of husband and wife leaving the hospital brought a lump of sentiment and affection to the collective throat of America. They were photographed holding hands—for shared strength, perhaps, for a physical expression of comfort, but perhaps also for the mutual courage they were able to give one another in their moment of tragedy. For the President, who was reticent about showing his feelings, this was a rare gesture. Looking at the picture, one had the feeling that in spite of heartache and nearly unbearable anguish, all was well between the President and the First Lady.

Over the years of their marriage, which was to spin its wheel of happiness and sorrow, joy and tragedy, misunderstandings and reconciliations over a decade, they embarked on an adventure in living that for fullness of experience has scarcely been equaled in our history.

What the people who had elected John F. Kennedy to the highest office in the land hadn't counted on was a bonus. This was a First Lady of such beauty, elegance, taste and culture that her effect during her husband's brief and tragically premature time of office was to influence, for the better, the culture of the country.

Suddenly, it became a status symbol to have written a book, or composed a symphony or painted a portrait. At the Inauguration, it was Robert Frost, the poet, who stood out among the politically oriented guests. For the American public, that takes such unabashed pleasure in criticizing and identifying with its greats, it has been a source of satisfaction to see the serenity, tenderness and understanding growing with the maturity of the First Family's marriage. In spite of tragedy, heartbreak, the irreparable loss of the children, particularly small Patrick whom the President had so dearly wanted, there were indications that this had become not only a good marriage but one with a suggestion of legendary grandeur that, out of the growth of its leading characters, would be sustained over their lives.

Among close friends, Mrs. Kennedy had the reputation for being a worrier. Whether this was a trait of loneliness or the prescience that sometimes comes to a sensitive nature, or a primitive need of appeasing the gods who had been so lavish with her, will never be known.

Scarcely three months later, her courage was to be tested again. But after that black morning in November, there was no steadfast husband to hold her hand and assuage her grief. There was, fortunately, her husband's brother Bobby, and the strength of his handclasp sustained her through the days which neither time nor mourning can ever completely erase.

After the birth and death of Patrick, Jacqueline Kennedy was ordered by her doctors to take a rest for several months. With the exception of a holiday that began in Greece, she had spent the time quietly, providing a happy home life for her husband and her children, Caroline and John.

A love of children was one of the durable links that not only bound Jacqueline and Jack Kennedy, but gave their future the promise of stature. The President was not a man who showed his private feelings to the world. What was deep within him was adroitly camouflaged by wit, humor and a mocking self-deprecation. It would seem natural that the sensitive, sickly boy raised in a climate of healthy exuberance, where competition was the order of the day, should raise an armor to shield his feelings and dreams from ridicule.

The Kennedy clan could both praise and deflate one another, and this atmosphere might not have been felicitous for the young dreamer. Perhaps as a result of a sickly childhood, Jack Kennedy kept his feelings to himself. Only now and then did one catch a glimpse of the sensitivity of the inner man. Nowhere was this more evident than in his attitude toward children in general, his own in particular. One of the most revealing insights into his personality is evident in the pictures of the President, Jacqueline and their first-born, Caroline, taken on the summer shore of Cape Cod. Here one is allowed a glimpse of the natural happiness and well-being of the President. For in playing with his tiny daughter, his own mischievous nature came into play. Jacqueline sitting crosslegged in the sand watches the tableau with the most luminous expression. It is more than a record of happy parents frolicking with their first-born. It is a key to the inner Jack Kennedy, and perhaps to the bond that was to grow daily stronger between him and his radiant young wife.

At any rate, the period of convalescence after Patrick's untimely birth and death was a time when Mrs. Kennedy was close to her husband and children.

For a while, it seemed to her that she could forget politics, which had never held much of an attraction for her. But when the President decided it was necessary to pay a visit to Texas—a state with twenty-five electoral votes that could play a decisive role in his campaign for re-election to the Presidency in 1964—she did not hesitate to accompany him. She had become since her trip to France a tremendous political asset to him. Then, too, these trips, whether in the interests of politics or statesmanship, were times when she could participate in the other part of his life—the part that so often kept him away from his family.

It was as though she had a premonition that this was an occasion when a wife should be with her husband.

The President's associates were not happy with the prospect of his Texas tour. It was basically a political visit. The civil rights issue had done much to wreck his political prestige. The President was aware of this, and even though his political intuition warned him against it, he marched with the forces of dignity and justice in fulfilling his pre-election promises.

Texas is a nest of extremists, some of them fanatic right-wingers. Adlai Stevenson had recently been shamefully mistreated in Dallas. Mr. Stevenson had even sent the President a warning to avoid Dallas. But on second thought, he withdrew it. He felt it unfair to judge an entire city by the misbehavior of a few extremists.

From the moment of the Kennedys' arrival in the Lone Star State, Jacqueline stole the show, as she had done on that memorable visit to France. The President humorously commented on this fact. When she was late in accompanying him to a breakfast sponsored by the Fort Worth Chamber of Commerce on the fateful November 22nd, he said, "Mrs. Kennedy is busy organizing herself. It takes a little longer, you know, but then she looks so much better than we do."

These are words that Jacqueline Kennedy will no doubt treasure all her days. They were spoken by a man visibly in love with his wife and proud of her stature as his mate.

At the same breakfast, the President said, "When I went to Paris, I once introduced myself as the man who accompanied Mrs. Kennedy, and I suppose I could introduce myself the same way here . . . nobody's interested in what Lyndon or I wear."

There was much applause for the smiling woman in the strawberry-pink suit with a pillbox hat to match.

Afterward, on the fan-jet Presidential plane, *Air Force One,* the President and the First Lady took off for Dallas.

It had been a dreary morning in Fort Worth, with a depressing rainfall. But the 2,500 guests at the breakfast were warm in their response to the President. And now, as the party, which included Governor and Mrs. John Connally, were airbound, the President made a few final changes in his Dallas speech.

He planned to say that "ignorance and misinformation" could "handicap this country's security." He meant to add that in a world of "complex and continuing problems, in a world of frustrations and irritations, America's leadership must be guided by the lights of learning and reason—or else those who confuse rhetoric with reality and the plausible with the possible will gain the popular ascendancy with their seemingly swift and simple solutions to every world problem."

It was one of his most eloquent speeches, and it was to end on a solemn warning: "We in this country, in this generation, are—by destiny rather than choice—the watchmen on the walls of world freedom. We ask, therefore, that we may be worthy of our power and responsibility—that we may exercise our strength with wisdom and restraint—and that we may achieve in our time and for all time the ancient vision of peace on earth, good will toward men. That must always be our goal—and the righteousness of our cause must always underlie our strength. For as it was written long ago, 'Except the Lord keep the city, the watchman waketh but in vain.' "

It was a speech he was never to deliver.

In Dallas, the sky was fresh and blue, the air newly washed and warm. The greetings of five thousand Texans at Love Field were gay with cheers and approval. The entire Texas trip seemed to be Jacqueline's show. People who crammed the airport and the streets in Texas cities seemed bent on catching sight of her. In her way, she had become the symbol of American royalty.

The President was to address a luncheon at the Trade Mart in downtown Dallas. It was a ten-mile trip through a cavern of applauding Texans who were showing a genuine affection for the President and his Lady. In the first car of the motorcade was the Presidential party. Governor Connally helped Jacqueline and his wife into their seats, then the President, and Connally got in himself. The Kennedys sat in the back seat, Jacqueline at her husband's left. The Governor and his lady took the jump seats in front of them. In the Number Two car sat heavily armed Secret Service men. The Number Three car was occupied by Vice President and Mrs. Lyndon Johnson and Senator Ralph Yarborough. Behind them came the hordes of press photographers, reporters, and local political dignitaries.

The fact that both women were wearing pink suits was something of an embarrassment to Mrs. Connally. But she forgot this in the cordial reception given the Kennedys. Her husband had been considerably worried about the temper of the city's hotheads. But the crowds were gay and friendly, their goodwill as sparkling as the morning sun. Nevertheless, it was something of an ordeal, especially since at the President's orders there was no bubble top to the car. There is no doubt that the Secret Service and the local officials would feel considerably relieved once the President stepped into the Trade Mart. They were all too conscious that leaflets branding the President, headlined "Wanted for Treason," had been handed out in the city. The Presidential party was in full sight and touch of the people lined up to cheer them and of the assassin who bided his time in the Dallas Book Repository.

The heat seemed overpowering. But soon now they would be in a pleasant, air-conditioned place.

The motorcycles that led the motorcade of the President of the United States chugged at a decreased rate of speed as they sighted Dallas' triple underpass. The Number One limousine slowed down for the left turn at the underpass.

Just then, Mrs. Connally turned from the jump seat to address John F. Kennedy. "Mr. President," she said with justifiable pride, "you can't say Dallas doesn't love you."

His answer, if any, was lost in the sound of a shot.

The President clutched his throat with both hands. A bullet, taking an almost vertical course, smashed its way through his neck above the necktie and then down into the chest.

Mrs. Connally felt certain that he was instantly dead. In an article in *McCall's* Magazine, "Since That Day in Dallas," she says that his face lost all animation. That instantly all vitality drained away from him.

This is in contradiction to the initial reports which suggested the first shot could not have been fatal. Or perhaps with all three shots coming together so swiftly, within a space of six seconds, it was impossible for her to judge whether the first or third shot was responsible for what she felt was instant death of the President. In that stunned moment, she was aware suddenly that her husband also was gravely hurt. The second bullet struck the Governor in the back, smashed through his chest, broke his wrist and ended in his thigh. He slumped bleeding to the floor, where his wife knelt beside him, stunned and shaken by dry wracking sobs.

At first Jacqueline Kennedy did not seem aware of what had happened. She turned to her right, not because of the cracks of a rifle, but because of the odd guttural sound emerging from her husband's throat. Only then did she scream, "Oh, my God, they've killed my husband! Jack! Jack!" He collapsed, falling against her shoulder, and she held his bleeding head in her protective arms.

She looked around, beseeching help. But the motorcade

kept going. In a frantic and touching search for someone to help, Jacqueline crawled out on the trunk of the car. As she crouched there, the President's head wound, bleeding profusely, left his life's blood on her skirt and stockings.

Finally a Secret Service man reached the rear of the car, leaped up and helped get the First Lady back to safety.

"Let's get out of here," a Secret Service agent told the police escort. "To the nearest hospital."

Speeding at seventy miles an hour, the driver of the Presidential car headed toward Parkland Memorial Hospital and arrived there nine minutes later.

Reporters followed in a car pool and reached the hospital almost simultaneously with the limousine. They saw the President lying face down in the back seat. They saw Mrs. Kennedy bent over him, holding his head, as a mother bends over a hurt child. They saw Governor Connally lying on the floor, blood staining his clothing, his wife cradling him gently in her arms. There was a stain of blood on the President's dark gray suit, and blood everywhere on the rear uphosltery.

Merriman Smith, the UPI White House reporter, ran over to Clint Hill, a Secret Service agent.

"How badly was he hit, Clint?" Merriman Smith asked.

"He's dead."

As stretchers were brought out to wheel both men into the emergency room, Jacqueline Kennedy clung to her outward composure. Governor Connally had to be assisted from the car first, for his big frame was blocking the way, and with a kind of superhuman strength, he lifted himself, so that the orderlies could get to the President. Mrs. Kennedy helped get her husband out of the car, and she rested a hand on his chest as he was wheeled into Emergency I.

The bouquet of red roses lay wilting among the drying blood in the President's limousine. . . .

Dr. Malcolm Perry was having salmon croquettes for lunch that day in the doctors' cafeteria. He was covering for Dr. Tom Shires, the hospital's chief resident in surgery.

When the call came in on the loudspeaker for Dr. Shires, the woman operator's voice added, "Stat," which meant an emergency. Dr. Perry took the telephone.

"President Kennedy has been shot," the operator said.

Emergency Room I has gray walls. It is a narrow room, and perhaps it suggested the shape of a coffin to those who peered into its door. There, in the middle of the room, on an aluminum hospital cart, lay the President of the United States. His chest was bare, and the wound at the back of his head was dripping blood to the floor.

Clinically, there was no sign of life.

The young doctor noticed the young woman in the pink suit standing against the gray tile wall. It was Jacqueline Kennedy, and her face was set in the cement of shock and self-discipline. Like Mrs. Connally, she was stained by her husband's blood. Once or twice during that time of anguish, the two women stared at each other. But their eyes were sightless. The vision of what they had recently seen was too awful to be comprehended.

Under the bright lights, Dr. Perry was working at a desperate pace to arouse some vestige of life in the President's body. There was no respiration. The chest lay white and quiet. But through the small bullet hole in the throat, air and blood were gathering in the chest. Dr. Perry decided to insert a tube in the windpipe. He worked without anesthesia. The President was not aware of pain. The third bullet had shattered the lower part of his brain, and he'd never been conscious since that awful moment.

Dr. Perry labored with the skill of a man who knows his job. But it was a battle lost before it was begun. Neither the tracheotomy nor the blood transfusions—of O negative blood—nor the attempt to stimulate the heart did any good. For ten minutes Dr. Perry massaged the chest of the President, pale and white and still in the terrible light, and Dr. Kemp Clark, Chief Neurosurgeon, in residency, watched the electrocardiogram intently for some sign of a heartbeat.

There was none.

The clock on the wall said one P.M.

It was November 22, 1963.

Time had run out for John Fitzgerald Kennedy, President of the United States.

Once, during those awful moments that seemed to stretch into eternity, Dr. Kemp Clark said to the young woman in the bloodstained suit, "Would you like to leave, ma'am? We can make you more comfortable outside."

"No," Jacqueline Kennedy said.

Someone had summoned a priest. He was Father Oscar Huber, and he and Jacqueline were moving toward the hospital cart where a white sheet had been drawn with tragic, unbelievable finality over that still white body. Now the priest pulled down the sheet so he could anoint the forehead of the dead President. Jacqueline Kennedy stood beside him while he held up his right hand and began the chant of the Roman Catholics for their dead.

"Si vivis, ego te absolvo a peccatis tuis. In nomine Patris et Filii et Spiritus Sancti. Amen."

With the holy oil on his thumb, the priest made a cross on the President's forehead. Then, having blessed the body once more, he prayed, "Eternal rest grant upon him, O Lord."

"And let perpetual light shine upon him," Jacqueline said softly.

They prayed together, and the reports are that she did not weep. From the moment the shots robbed her and the nation of its leader, she had summoned some deep strength, a kind of spiritual armor that was to make her behavior in the following days a model of grieving deportment for an agonized world.

"A hundred yards, and the President would have been out of the reach of the assassin's bullet," reporters mourned.

But safety was not destined for him. Perhaps it was a part of the course of history that, like another great President, he was destined to be sacrificed toward a goal beyond the grasp of those grieving and unreconciled.

Perhaps at that moment, out of the deep freeze of shock and horror, Jacqueline Kennedy recalled the passage from Ecclesiastes which was one of her husband's favorites:

"For everything there is a season, and a time for every matter under heaven:

"A time to be born and a time to die . . ."

She did not leave him. It was as though she could not grasp the harsh, shattering reality of it.

Father Huber had said the prayer, "If you are living, I absolve you from your sins. . . ."

Father Huber had said, "I am convinced that his soul had not left his body."

She remained with him, through the long ordeal ahead, as though he was still a living extension of herself. She was with him when the casket arrived in a hearse. It was a bronze casket and it was heavy.

The President had been a big man.

Death is not the only occasion that wants mourning. In the checks and balances, the pluses and minuses that make up the pattern of life, the time of achievement is invariably followed by a period of depression. Even if the victim is unaware of it, there is the blue mood, the listlessness, the inability to participate again in the mainstream of life.

In spite of the glamor and romantic aspects of Jacqueline Kennedy, there had been many moments of gravity and mourning for her. The divorce of her parents, which divided her loyalties . . . at eleven, even the most resourceful child is hard put to cope with such realities. A depression, even unrecognized, is often inevitable. There was the birth and death of her first two children, where surely a post partum time of mourning was part of her convalescence. There was the tragedy of young Patrick's death, after life seemed assured to him, and in all of her pregnancies there was the added trauma of the Caesarian section.

But there was nothing compared to the loss of her husband.

Even in the moment of shock, however, when her reactions were mechanical and perhaps disoriented, years of conditioned reflexes came to her rescue. Her growing appreciation of her husband's place in the history of his country took precedence over her grief for the man who was her beloved.

In Emergency I, with the covered body of the man who was her husband, his blood still in a pool on the floor under the hospital cart, she was transformed from the grieving wife into a woman of such dignity and stature that her role has been likened to that of the heroic women of the Greek mythology.

Not once after the realization of her husband's death did she lose her composure. It was as though she knew that this was what he would have expected of her—that it was how the widow of a martyred President must act.

Before the casket arrived in Emergency I, she took her wedding ring off her hand and placed it on her dead husband's finger. She meant no bravado by the gesture. It was the simple impulse of a woman who inwardly knew that even death could not sever the bonds of their feelings. Then she kissed his lips and waited for his casket to be closed. With her hand resting on the casket, she walked out to the hearse.

Not once, through the excruciating ordeal of the swearing-in of Lyndon Johnson as the new President of the United States, the flight back in *Air Force One,* the trip to Bethesda Naval Hospital, the night of waiting for his body to be prepared for its final repose, did her poise and courage and thoughtfulness for others show a sign of self-pity. Her discipline was soldierly, but one was aware of a deep withdrawal, as though she was summoning all her inner resources to see her through the role she must carry—the role that would go down in history as a fitting threnody for her husband's martyrdom.

Before *Air Force One* took off, she joined the group waiting in the plane's gold-carpeted lounge to see Lyndon Johnson sworn in by Judge Sarah T. Hughes as the thirty-sixth President of the United States.

It was hot in the lounge. But if Jacqueline suffered, there was no evidence of it. Her pink pillbox hat was gone, her dark hair fell around her face, but the jacket was neatly buttoned. She watched the proceedings with her face lowered, the eyes fixed on the ceremony, but the jaw was close to her chest. It was a habit that was to become a part of her in future months.

After kissing Jacqueline and his wife, the new President quietly took command: "Okay, let's get this plane back to Washington." For in that time of confusion, there was fear of a conspiracy to assassinate all top United States officials.

Lady Bird Johnson clasped Jacqueline's cold hand and whispered, "The whole nation mourns your husband."

Dallas Police Chief J. E. Curry was gentle with the young widow. "God bless you, little lady," he said, "but you ought to go back and lie down."

Mrs. John F. Kennedy forced a smile. She said, "No, thanks. I'm fine."

All the way back to Andrews Air Force Base near Washington, she sat by her husband's body in the rear of the plane. With her were Presidential Assistants Lawrence O'Brien, Kenneth O'Donnell, David Powers and Air Force Aide Brigadier General Godfrey McHugh.

"What's to become of all of you?" she asked. "What are you going to do?"

O'Brien was to say later: "We were supposed to be the tough ones. But this frail girl turned out to have more strength than any of us."

The new President was solicitous of Mrs. Kennedy's welfare. Politely she refused offers of help. She said she just wanted to sit by the casket. There she was to remain during the flight.

During this sorrowful journey that was to take the body of

John F. Kennedy back to the airport he had left so recently as a vital and active man, the new President dictated his first public statement.

"This is a sad time for all people. We have suffered a loss that cannot be weighed. For me it is a deep personal tragedy. I know the world shares the sorrow that Mrs. Kennedy and her family bear. I will do my best. That is all I can do. I ask for your help—and God's."

The news that stunned the world, leaving it emotionally shattered, had a telling effect on the Kennedys. But although they were the close-knit, unique family of whom the late President was justifiably proud, there was none of the mourning of an Irish wake. The family kept their grief within the bosom of their unit. To the world they showed the same dignity and composure that had become a symbol of the newly widowed Jacqueline.

Bob Kennedy had brought U.S. Attorney Robert Morgenthau home for lunch, when at 1:44 P.M. a message came for him. J. Edgar Hoover was on the wire. Bob's wife, Ethel, saw by his reaction that something was horribly wrong. After he hung up, no words came from his lips. Finally, he was able to speak.

"Jack's been shot. It may be fatal."

Yet after the initial shock, the Kennedy strength came to the fore. The Attorney General spent the afternoon doing what needed to be done. Members of the clan, Ted and Eunice, were dispatched to Hyannis Port to be with their parents. Sargent Shriver was delegated to make the arrangements for the burial. Twice during that anguished afternoon, Bobby telephoned his mother. During the intervals between activities, he seemed to lose himself in a private and terrible grief.

But when it was time for *Air Force One* to arrive at Andrews Air Force Base, he straightened his shoulders.

Now was his time to help Jacqueline.

He came home for the last time.

It was cool in Washington that night, and the mist gave a bone-chilling bite to the air. The pilot set his plane, with its tragic and precious burden, skillfully on the field. There was silence, a silence more terrible than wailing. In the dark field, with its piercing floodlights, the hush was unnatural and ghostly. A white cargo lift was rolled out to meet the plane. A man opened the door and looked out.

The first man out was Larry O'Brien, and then came Dave Powers and Kenny O'Donnell, the beloved members of what John F. Kennedy called with ironic humor his "Irish Mafia."

It was their custom to accompany the President, and now they brought him back, and an honor guard of six Marines reached out to receive the coffin.

Only the broadcasters were audible, and even their voices were hushed as they talked into their microphones. Then Jacqueline came out of the plane, and Bobby Kennedy raised his arms to assist her. They embraced quietly, but neither wept. Bobby guided her toward the gray service ambulance and into the interior where the casket was resting. Then he got in, and the ambulance disappeared into the dark of night.

Behind it were left the men who had served John Fitzgerald Kennedy valorously, with the devotion he inspired in all peace-loving men. Ted Sorensen, who was perhaps intellectually closer to him than any other; Arthur Schlesinger, McGeorge Bundy, Hubert Humphrey, Mike Mansfield, and Everett Dirksen of Congress. The shock had united antifriends and factions into a unit of awareness of what a loss they and the country had sustained.

It was appropriate that a guard of sailors awaited the arrival of the dead President who had once been of their number. A hush seemed to hang over the darkness as the body arrived at Bethesda Naval Hospital.

During that endless night, Jacqueline maintained her supernatural calm. Friends have since reported that not once during that awful vigil, while her husband's body was being prepared for burial, did she break down. Hers was a private grief, discernible only to those intimate with her. For the world, which offered her the token of sympathy and sorrow, she courageously maintained her own composure. It was the miracle that kept others from emotional collapse.

Her mother, Mrs. Hugh Auchincloss, had told the children earlier that evening of their father's death. But it fell to their mother to relate it in greater detail the next morning. Then, dressed in mourning, but keeping her children in identical pale blue coats, Jacqueline took them to the East Room of the White House, where the casket reposed. Here a Roman Catholic mass was held for the family and a few friends. John-John, as his father had affectionately called him, was in the corridor with his nurse, Maude Shaw. He complained of being lonely; there was no one to play with him.

Jacqueline Kennedy was in rigid control of herself. Earlier that morning, in the cold gray hours of dawn at Bethesda Hospital, she had said to Mrs. Evelyn Lincoln, the late President's devoted secretary, "It's getting late, and I'm going to be here quite a while, so why don't you go home and try to get some rest? You hold up for the next few days and then we'll all collapse."

All through that dawn, Jacqueline, although still in a state of shock, had planned the details of her husband's funeral. The similarity between his tragic death and that of Abraham Lincoln was not lost upon her. A friend was called and asked to go to the upstairs library in the White House, where there was a special book of photographs and drawings connected with Lincoln's lying-in-state and his funeral ceremonies. Jacqueline said she wished everything to be as similar as possible to Lincoln's services. Even the catafalque on which the casket would lie was exactly to duplicate Lincoln's. She supervised the preparations for the hanging of the mourning drapes and arranging the catafalque.

"Couldn't the Honor Guard include a member of the Special Forces?" she asked. For she knew of her husband's respect for the green-bereted troops who had served with such distinction in Vietnam. Her wish was granted.

During the first day of her grief, Mrs. Kennedy's thoughtfulness far exceeded any obligations of her position. This was a genuine from-the-heart gesture. She called her brother-in-law, Attorney-General Kennedy, and suggested that he telephone and give her condolences to the wife of Officer J. D. Tippitt, who had been shot by Lee Harvey Oswald.

"What that poor woman must be going through," Mrs. Kennedy said.

Lee Harvey Oswald, named as the assassin, was a loner. He had been a misfit most of his life. The need to show his anger at the unappreciative world grew like a cancerous thing in the dark, sick region of his brain. In order to show that he was as good as anybody, even better ("I am the commander!" he is reported to have snapped at his gentle frightened wife), he had to do something so big that it would startle and astound the whole world.

The news that John Fitzgerald Kennedy would visit Dallas was the coincidence, the fragment that contributed to the weird mosaic of Oswald's needs. Once he had attempted, according to later admissions of his Russian wife, to kill retired General Edwin Walker, a right-wing extremist. He had even acknowledged a plan to assassinate Richard Nixon, which was aborted when Nixon canceled plans to visit Texas.

But now there was to be the perfect victim.

Under the open window of the sixth floor of the Dallas Book Repository, police were to discover three spent cartridges and one not used. They found the weapon, too, a sawed-off .30 caliber rifle of Italian make, fitted with a four-power telescopic sight.

Ironically, Lee Harvey Oswald and his wife, Marina, and their two children were living in Texas through the Christian charity of a Quaker, Mrs. Ruth Paine. Oswald had once admitted, on a radio panel show called "Carte Blanche," to being a Marxist, and he spoke warmly of the Fair Play for Cuba Committee. Yet even the left-wingers had little to do with him. His behavior evidently marked him as a difficult and isolated personality.

It was his recent custom to visit his pregnant wife and daughter only on weekends. But the Thursday before the Black Friday, he showed up unexpectedly at the little suburban house of Mrs. Paine. With the simplicity that marked her faith, Mrs. Paine had opened her heart to the plight of Oswald's Russian wife, who was pregnant, and burdened now with one small child and a husband out of work. Yet her very Christian act was part of the over-all pattern in the act of senseless violence that caused the untimely death of the young President. For it was in her home that Lee Harvey Oswald had his coffee that Friday morning and from her garage he picked up the rifle, wrapped in paper, that was to fire the shots.

Michael Paine, Ruth's husband, had often tried to reason with Lee Oswald. But Lee was apparently highly opinionated and incapable of a deviation from the opinions he'd picked up in his Communist readings. His I.Q., incidentally, was reported to be 103, which is about average and doesn't amount to the intellectual equipment of a thinking man. He was a bitter, hostile mouthpiece for what had been preached over the years in Red countries.

Thursday night, during his unexpected visit to the Paine home, Mrs. Paine noticed that he had gone out to the garage. He had left on the light. But she thought nothing of it, since the Oswalds' books and scraps of household wares were stored there.

Lee was already gone Friday morning when Mrs. Paine got up at seven thirty to make breakfast. Mrs. Paine and Marina Oswald sat in the living room around noon, watching on TV the Presidential arrival in the Dallas airport. The news of the assassination deeply shocked both women.

Mrs. Paine has since reported that Marina Oswald had said, "What a terrible thing this is for Mrs. Kennedy! How sad it is that her children will have to grow up without a father!"

"I only cried twice," Caroline Kennedy said gravely to one of her classmates. . . .

"I wish I weren't going to Dallas," President Kennedy said three days before his assassination.

This is what Pierre Salinger, the President's former White House Secretary, reported approximately eight months later, on July 27, 1964, in Tokyo, a stopover on a world tour.

Mr. Salinger went on to explain that it was "not because of any fear of going there, but because of a weariness from the press of his duties."

Tears are given to us for a purpose; they are perhaps Nature's way of healing wounds that seem impossible to heal. But there were no tears in Jacqueline Kennedy's eyes as she went through the ritual of the final ceremonies to mark one of the most tragic events of our time.

The assassination brought with it disbelief, shock, grief—and a kind of nationally shared guilt.

It was as though in our horror at looking inward, at the affluent society that nourished such extremists, we were muttering *mea culpa*. But it was already too late. Two of our great Presidents, men who had faith in the freedom they preached, had died for it, victims of disturbed personalities. President Kennedy's assassin harbored hate without personal direction. A vicious, unquenched rebellion against order and authority brewed its poisons in the mind of that pale, sharp-featured, immature person. By contrast, President Kennedy had enormous patience and tolerance. He was a man who trusted reason and logic, and perhaps because of this could not understand the behavior of either extreme right- or left-wingers.

Were any of these reflections in Jacqueline Kennedy's

mind as she stood frozen in the gray-tiled emergency room? Or were there the vivid vignettes of the last years of their marriage which grew into a dazzling radiant mature love that was to bring both husband and wife such deep inner joy?

Neither she nor her husband bore the remotest resemblance to the rags-to-riches American dream that was prevalent a couple of generation ago. Yet both of them, children of the rich, helped to bring a new facet to the White House—an image of taste and culture that seemed to put the nation artistically on a par with European countries. But more than this, her husband, with his youth, vitality, sincerity, and passionate dedication for peace had inspired around the world a kind of respect and affection that it has been given few of our Presidents to know. John F. Kennedy had been inspired with a selfless devotion to mankind; and in its mourning, mankind returned his devotion.

Churches were filled with prayers for his soul. Men and women who had never known him but felt a close kinship wept openly in the streets.

In Milan, an Italian flag hung at half mast beside the spire of a cathedral. Italian President Antonio Segni, too ill to fly to Washington, went to Mass in Rome and could not control his sobs.

In a Roman church, composer Igor Stravinsky conducted a performance of his *Mass for Mixed Chorale,* in a gesture of respect for the late President.

The Union Jack hung at half mast over the houses of Parliament in London. Commons made a gesture that is usually given only to the death of royalty and prime ministers. It adjourned.

West Berlin demonstrated the most moving spectacle outside of Washington. There was a march by torchlight of thousands of mourners, and the square where the President had spoken during his June visit (*"Ich bin ein Berliner"*) was rechristened the John F. Kennedy Platz.

Pope Paul VI knelt at the foot of his throne and offered a special prayer for the soul of John F. Kennedy.

In Ballykelly Church in Ireland, the priest said to his kneeling parish, "Never again will we see his smiling face."

And from the Irish poet, Dominic Behan, came the poignant lines:

> "What lips will smile so gay, laughing their fears away,
> Who will lead the fray, Son of the Gael?"

Not only nations, but the people who make up the nations, were bowed in grief. Office workers in the government who were carrying out the designs of government which the late President and his staff had planned were stunned into a state of shock. They moved silently through the long halls of the government buildings, looking at each other, as though from someone would come the miraculous word that it was all a child's nightmare, and that on the next day, JFK would descend from *Air Force One* with his lightness and grace, a quip on his lips.

In Cleveland, where Ringling Brothers, Barnum and Bailey Circus was giving a performance, the stars and working men, many of them from the Continent, burst into tears. A service was held for the President before each performance.

Everywhere, people met in a mutual sense of loss. Eyes were red-rimmed. Tears flowed in a burst of sorrow that did not differentiate between men and women. The awfulness of it would take time to penetrate the soul, but meanwhile the anguish showed itself in a universal display of sorrow, the like of which had not been seen in the land.

"I hurt," a young girl said, holding her chest.

The whole country hurt. The whole world hurt. . . .

The night of his nomination, John Fitzgerald Kennedy had said, "All of us are united . . . in our devotion to this country."

He served two years, ten months and two days.

And at the moment of his burial it was as though the world itself, united in its burden of grief for the young warrior, had dedicated itself unconsciously toward fulfilling his vision of world peace.

That she herself had been inches away from death in that moment of tragedy evidently never occurred to Jacqueline Kennedy. Now the spirit that seemed to take over, lulling the shock and grief, was the sudden awareness of similarity between the death of her husband and that of Lincoln. From that moment on, she seemed to marshal some fantastic inner resources that gave her the strength and dignity to fulfill what she knew now was her own sacred mission.

With the help of Henry Suydam, chief of *Life* Magazine's Washington Bureau, she began arranging the innumerable painstaking details that would ensure for John F. Kennedy a burial like that of the first martyred President.

When the chill gray dawn of November 23rd bleached

the dark, she brought back her husband's body to the White house, where it was to lie in state in the East Room. Only after she had attended the details did she see her children for the first time. Before noon, she returned to the East Room for the special family Mass. Then, for the first time, did she consent to rest.

While she was in temporary seclusion from the eyes of the nation, the final dramatic moments were spinning out in Dallas. Lee Harvey Oswald, the man accused of assassinating her husband, was himself shot to death by Jack Ruby, a man obsessed with grief and violence.

Sunday morning, while the casket was carried out of the White House and brought by an honor guard to the Rotunda of the Capitol, Mrs. Kennedy, in black, and holding each child by the hand, followed the bier up the thirty-six marble steps. In the Rotunda, the children still at her side, Jacqueline Kennedy maintained her stoic calm, although several times it seemed to onlookers close by that she swayed.

Caroline, at six, seemed aware of the significance of the ceremonies, and her young face took on an expression of gravity and sorrow that has often characterized it since.

Young John-John was in the mood for friendliness, and he was hurried out of the Rotunda.

With a dignity so exquisite that it could not fail to move those watching, Mrs. Kennedy and Caroline walked to the flag-covered casket to kneel beside it.

Jacqueline Kennedy's faith had matured during the years of her marriage. It was often said the President was a "Fifth Avenue Catholic," that while his feeling for religion was deep, ritual had less meaning for him than for his wife.

This would seem consistent with her character. The strain of the devout French was latent within her spirit; earlier it showed itself in the grace of her artistic endeavors. But under stress, it began to take the concrete form that was to fashion her into the mold of a devout believer. She had married into a family that took its religion as part of daily routine, and once she became indoctrinated her whole being seemed to be infused with an identity to the solemn and beautiful rituals of the Church.

She was consulted on each minute detail of the final burial plans. Now, a sense of what would go down in history, to be read and studied generations later, helped her contain her private grief.

On that chilly Saturday evening, when 250,000 mourners passed the bier to pay their last respects to John F. Kennedy, Jacqueline asked Robert Kennedy to take her back there again. It was as though she couldn't stay away; as though the strands that should be severed by death had instead grown stronger; as though she knew the brevity of the time the mortal remains would be with her. Mid-evening, she knelt again by the bier, gently put her lips to the flag. Then she stood up. For a moment, she looked around her, at the silent mourners waiting patiently in line, the sound of their feet a soft dirge. Robert touched her arm, and she seemed to rouse herself. Out in the cold night air, he led her toward a waiting limousine. But she shook her head.

"Let me walk," she said. "Let me walk."

Perhaps in the pictures that unreeled beneath the numbed feeling was the memory of those walks on the sand dunes of Cape Cod, with the wild grasses and the wild berries and the wind and salt air and sun and the distant horizon.

In the crowd, a woman recognized her. With an impulse that was an expression of a nation's feeling, she approached. Impulsively, she enfolded Jacqueline Kennedy in her arms. Without words, Jacqueline returned the embrace. Then she walked on, blind, without outer clothes in the winter cold and dark. But when the crowds recognized her, she had to go back to her car.

Among the many eloquent tributes to Jacqueline Kennedy was the one from Senator Mike Mansfield of Montana, Majority Leader of the United States Senate.

"There was a sound of laughter, and in a moment, it was no more. And so, she took a ring from her finger and placed it in his hands. . . .

"There was a father with a little boy, a little girl, and a joy of each in the other. In a moment, it was no more, and so she took a ring from her finger and placed it in his hands. . . .

"There was a husband who asked much and gave much, and out of the giving and the asking, wove with a woman what could not be broken in life, and in a moment, it was no more. And so she took a ring from her finger, and placed it in his hands, and kissed him and closed the lid of the coffin. . . ."

Monday, the day of national mourning, the day of the funeral, the slain President's body was to be taken from the care of the Guard of Honor and brought to its final resting place at Arlington Cemetery.

Jacqueline Kennedy walked behind the body of her husband for six long blocks from the White House to Saint Matthew's Cathedral. Although Robert and Teddy Kennedy were on either side of her, she did not need support. Her head was erect, her set face hidden by the veil of mourning, but her stride was long and her manner had a kind of heroic dignity that had marked her every action since the terrible moment in Dallas.

The caisson on which the flag-covered casket rested was drawn by three pairs of matched gray horses. The riderless horse, carrying the black boots reversed in the stirrups followed. It was a symbol of the dead warrior who would never ride again. There were the muffled drums and the shrill wailing pipes, and behind them marched the great of the world who had come to pay homage to the man who truly cared for an enduring peace.

Within the Cathedral, there was Cardinal Cushing to say the low funeral Mass. It was the Cardinal, the old and influential friend of the Kennedys, who had married Jacqueline Bouvier and John Fitzgerald Kennedy a decade before and who had later played such a warm, paternal, religious role in their lives. He had christened Caroline and John-John, and had buried Patrick Bouvier Kennedy only three months previously. Luigi Vena who had sung "Ave Maria" at their wedding was to sing it today again.

Only in the Cathedral did Jacqueline Kennedy break. But it was a brief moment, and miraculously she had herself in control again. It was a few minutes later, waiting outside, that John-John saluted. He did not quite comprehend what it was all about, but there were soldiers and drums and martial music and flags, and always when he had been with his father during ceremonies, he had seen that it was proper to salute. So now he carried out his teachings proudly, no doubt feeling that his father would be pleased with him.

The children were sent back to the White House to spare them the ordeal of the burial services. During the hour it took to reach Arlington National Cemetery, the sun eased the chill in the air. Military units took position before the grave. The grave site was a small hill in front of the Custis-Lee house. In the distance was the Lincoln Memorial.

It was an odd whim of fate that earlier in the year, one

day in March, John F. Kennedy had come to Arlington with a friend. He had looked toward the view of Washington, dazzling in the early spring sun, and he had said, "I could stay here forever."

The Kennedy family took the seats that were placed beside the grave. Theirs too was a collective dignity and restraint. After fifty jet fighters roared over the cemetery, *Air Force One* flew by, dipping its wings in farewell to its gallant Chief.

A cardinal committed the dead President to the keeping of Christ. Taps, the most mournful of all sounds, echoed in the soft air. The Honor Guard folded the flag that had graced the coffin and gave it to Mrs. Kennedy. She came forward and lit what was to be the Eternal Flame. Then she turned. For a moment, as she walked, it seemed as if she were about to lose her balance. But she caught herself. She walked away from the grave, her hand clasped in Robert Kennedy's.

The good manners that were so much a part of her upbringing and the thoughtful attention to others were not lost in her own anguish. After the funeral, she graciously received the great who had come to do her late husband homage. In the next few days, she was to write personal notes of gratitude to every member of the White House staff. There were about 114 of them, and they included the housemen, laundresses and janitors.

As the shock and numbness wore off, Jacqueline Kennedy was to recall some of her husband's favorite quotations. They were from the musical comedy *Camelot,* and she remembered how, late at night, before they went to sleep, he would play some of the *Camelot* pieces.

"Don't let it be forgot, that once there was a spot, for one brief shining moment that was known as Camelot."

If this too had taken place briefly in our country, it was forged out of the character of a frail sickly young boy who had read stories of valor and of a delicate girl who had loved animals as passionately as humans, and of these two who had come together and out of their life had given the country one beautiful and shining moment.

In his book *Profiles in Courage,* which was to win for John F. Kennedy a Pulitzer Prize, but more importantly to give people an inkling of the man they were one day to elect to the highest office in the land, he wrote:

The courage of life is often a less dramatic spectacle than the courage of a final moment; but it is no less than a magnificent mixture of triumph and tragedy. A man does what he must—in spite of personal consequences, in spite of obstacles and dangers and pressures—and that is the basis of all human morality.

It was a book that he had dedicated to Jacqueline, his wife.

Chapter Two

In order to follow the story of a love that has become a legend in its time, of a sensitive, poetic woman who was transformed by an act of senseless violence into a figure of heroic stature, we must trace the beginnings of the three figures who moved toward their destiny that brilliant sun-drenched day in Dallas.

Thomas Mann once said, "Character is fate."

To understand the directions of fate that brought these three together in a rendezvous of assassination and death, it is necessary to explore their backgrounds, to pinpoint the happiness and misery, serenity and stress that contributed to the formation of their personalities.

All three—two men and a woman—were born well into the twentieth century. Their coming together in bleak and bitter climax in the white heat and black tensions of a city in Texas may well change the course of our country's future.

There is the second son of a noisy, energetic Irish-American family. Ill health made him something of a maverick. He evidently attracted to his frail body all known childhood viruses. Left to his own resources, he might have squandered his adolescence in dreams rather than action. He was fascinated by the legendary heroes of the past. Since children tend to identify with their idols, his eager admiration for courage and valor may have contributed to his own sense of destiny.

But he had, also, a father image that was ambitious, ruthless and pragmatic.

The boy's name was John Fitzgerald Kennedy. He was born on May 29, 1917, in Brookline, Massachusetts, to Rose and Joseph Kennedy. He came from a family of politics and modest affluence; a family driven by the goals that motivate an immigrant clan to achieve acceptance in a new milieu.

The boy's father, Joe Kennedy, was thin-skinned only where the snubs of the Proper Bostonians were concerned. As a result, he inspired his expanding brood with an ambitious and competitive spirit rarely seen in one family. It was to have finally the cumulative power of an atomic bomb.

Twenty-two years later, on October 18, 1939, another boy was born to another family. A photograph taken of him at the age of two reveals a handsome, plump child in a dark jumper and white shirt. His blond hair is combed over his head in a fat sausage curl. There is an open, affectionate gleam in his eyes. His smile shows none of the sneering cynicism that was to distort his later pictures. He looks like a pleasant little boy from a comfortable middle-income family.

He was christened Lee Harvey Oswald.

He was born to Mrs. Marguerite Claverie Oswald. At the time of his birth, his father was already two months dead. Was it perhaps the need of a father that contributed much to the boy's anger and hostility during the growing years—and impelled him, twenty-four years later, to slaughter the man who was symbolically the father image of his country?

Of these three, the woman came of age in her own time, but not in circumstances of her choosing.

The women whom we remember best with admiration and reverence are often thrust into history at a psychological moment that brings into full splendor those heroic traits that arouse the awe of people. It was this way with the woman who was in her frivolous time the Debutante of the Year and became for all of us the symbol of dignity and fortitude in the black despairing moments of grief.

She was born Jacqueline Lee Bouvier and she took her time about making her entrance into the world. The date was June 28, 1929, and the event took place, in an impromptu manner, at a hospital near the Bouvier summer home in Southampton. She was a heavy baby, weighing eight pounds; six weeks overdue, she was unusually well developed for an infant.

She was the first-born of a handsome, favored couple who had everything going for them. Money, social position, good looks—all contributed to make the Jack Bouviers the status symbols of their time.

John Vernou Bouvier III was thirty-six before he decided that marriage to dark, slim and intensely feminine

Janet Lee was preferable to the life of a perennial and popular socialite bachelor. Janet was twenty, and Jack was sixteen years her senior, when they fell in love.

It is perhaps a commentary on Jacqueline's admiration for her parents that she followed their pattern. Her own husband, John Fitzgerald Kennedy, was an eligible bachelor of thirty-seven, who had no concrete plans for a life of matrimony when he first met her, and she was thirteen years his junior. One wonders why these handsome, dynamic men usually take brides so much younger than themselves, girls so utterly and enchantingly feminine.

It was in East Hampton, where Janet Lee spent her teenage summers, that she first met Jack Bouvier. Janet was the daughter of the James T. Lees, and children of the family numbered three devastatingly beautiful daughters. The Lees gave each girl her own car, which lent a certain *cachet* to her allure which the young men of the resort readily acknowledged. Janet was already a skillful horsewoman. Perhaps all the energy and inner drive that could not find a suitable outlet in the easy, comfortable and yet conformist resort living showed itself in her daring and skill on a horse.

The summer after her debut at a dance at Sherry's, Janet began to find favor with Jack Bouvier. She was no longer the small energetic friend of his young twin sisters, but an exceedingly lovely and feminine creature in her own right.

It couldn't have been easy for a man of Jack Bouvier's background and experience to decide on a permanent alliance. He was unbelievably handsome and understandably spoiled by women. He had the dark, intense good looks and the heavy tan that gave him a suggestion of Continental parentage. His friends at Yale called him The Sheik, and he was often mistaken by strangers for Clark Gable.

The Bouvier family, with whose genealogy Jacqueline Kennedy has a happy affinity, is closely associated with France. Several generations back, the first Bouvier came to America where his unit took part in the British surrender at Yorktown. He was André Eustache Bouvier, aged twenty-one, and he came from an ancient family in Fontaine, near Grenoble, France. He had enlisted in the Grenoble Artillery Regiment. Unfortunately, his regiment's roster was lost, so his name was not officially recorded. After fighting for the Americans under General Lafayette, together with twenty-four other Bouviers, André returned to Southern France and settled in Pont-St. Esprit, where he married Therese Mercier.

Although André Bouvier never again visited America, his son, Michel, Jacqueline's great-great-grandfather, did. Michel's brother, Joseph, remained behind in Pont-St. Esprit where today his descendants are proud of their distant kinship to America's former First Lady.

Michel left the family home while still a young lad, capturing the attention of Napoleon's brother, Joseph Bonaparte, King of Spain. After Napoleon's defeat, the exiled Joseph made his home in Bordentown, New Jersey. Michel soon followed Joseph to America and settled in Philadelphia, where he married Louise Vernou, daughter of a nobleman who had fled his native France during the Revolution.

Michel prospered as a marble importer and manufacturer of veneer. He died a rich man. Philadelphia, proud of its adopted son, named a street after him—Bouvier Street.

Among the children of Michel and Louise was the first John Vernou Bouvier, Jacqueline's great-grandfather, who married Caroline Ewing of Philadelphia, for whom Jacqueline's daughter is named. Caroline Bouvier established the New York Foundling Hospital. Here, unwanted children, without respect to race, color or creed, can find a haven. A collateral ancestor of Jacqueline's, Mother Katharine Drexel, founded a religious order dedicated toward helping Indians and Negroes.

From the very beginning, the pleasures of cosmopolitan living in the Bouvier family was given character by a strong sense of religious faith and possibly the masochistic need that is often a subterranean trait in the saintly.

By the time John Vernou Bouvier III met Janet Lee, he had a seat on the Stock Exchange.

Janet's family was involved in New York real estate and banking, so it was evident that the young married couple would not want for security.

The wedding of Jacqueline Kennedy's parents took place July 7, 1928, at St. Philomena's Church in East Hampton. It was the social spectacular of the season. Janet's slender, small figure was swathed in satin, silver and a magnificent wedding veil. Her bridesmaids reflected the lovely summer day in their green chiffon frocks that dipped low in back, and their yellow wide-brimmed hats. At the high-noon reception, Meyer Davis' orchestra played for five hundred guests and the radiant couple began their honeymoon on the *Aquitania.*

The Lee-Bouvier wedding was in keeping with the frivolous years before the Black Thursday of the Stock Market turned American economy into the shambles that was to last until the onset of World War II. Whether the young couple found it necessary to trim their sails in the following years is not evidenced by their standard of living. Janet's father, James E. Lee, gave them their first permanent living quarters—a duplex on Park Avenue.

Here Jacqueline was brought home as an infant. From this apartment she was taken, in the Lee family christening gown from Paris—which Caroline Kennedy was later to use—to the beautiful Church of St. Ignatius Loyola in New York City. The time was three days before Christmas. Her godfather was her nine-year-old cousin, Michel Bouvier, whose father had died a short while before.

Jacqueline was a sturdy child, high-spirited, roguish and independent. There is a revealing formal portrait of her in Mary Van Rensselaer Thayer's definitive biography, published by Doubleday and Company. Jacqueline at three going on four gave promise of a dark, unique beauty. The resemblance between her and her father is marked, with the same rich dark hair that seemed to have a life of its own; the long dark eyebrows over eyes as wide-spaced as a delicate animal's; the blunt nose, and the full wide mouth divided between discipline and willfulness. The image reflected is that of an exquisite doll but with a very human mind and will. The large head, the face with a promise of squareness are more marked in a later photograph taken with her father. Here Jackie, in riding clothes, sits on her horse while her father holds the reins. There is pride and humor in his attitude, and fierce intense adoration in the child's. Her father was Jackie's first great love, and possibly the one person from whom she never held herself aloof.

Training for a social life began early for Jackie. A party for her second birthday—while she was still the only child in the family—found her a warm and friendly little hostess, willing to share her toys and pony rides with twenty little guests.

At two years of age, she also made her first appearance at a dog show in East Hampton with her pet, a black Scotty named Hootchie. She often took him for a run in Central

Park, both of them guarded by her nurse, Bertha Newey. Strollers must have been enchanted by the sight of the small, sturdy child dressed in a pale blue woolen coat and leggings, her rather large head protected by a blue bonnet with a feminine frill of pink, her hands in immaculate white gloves neatly holding the puppy's leash.

Jacqueline's love for dogs and horses has never changed; a home without livestock of assorted shapes and breeds would have been unbearable for her. It is fortunate that John Fitzgerald Kennedy also liked animals.

According to an article in the July 19, 1964, issue of *The New York Times,* pets play an important part in shaping a child's personality. Through his pet, new avenues of experience open up to the youngster. It is even easier for a child to adapt himself to the trauma of death in someone near him, when he has first experienced the death of a beloved animal.

Often family pets reflect the emotional climate of the family. The behavior patterns of dogs and cats may mirror the tensions of their own owners.

To Jacqueline, animals have always assumed the role of friends. She appears to have established an extrasensory form of communication with them which she has bequeathed to her children. The legendary tenderness of the mature Jacqueline Kennedy may have had its origin in her childish tender love for her pets.

That she kept her pet rabbit in the bathtub was a source of amusement for her father, who was enormously understanding and indulgent with the daughter who shaped up so much like himself.

Jackie's childhood was busy, active, filled with challenges beyond those of an average girl. She got lost in Central Park, and when a policeman found her, she told him calmly that it was her nurse who was lost. She was a year old when her mother first sat her astride a pony. She learned to jump low fences with astonishing skill and a premature courage. She was an early reader, and like the boy who was to grow up to become her husband, she read voraciously. Many books were beyond her age, yet to her mother's astonishment and her father's awe, she grasped their meaning. She was an extraordinary confident child, fearless, outgiving, with many evidences of a colorful extrovert.

No matter how much a small girl may adore her male parent, it is usually the mother she emulates. This is all to the good, for in the transition from child to woman, it is particularly important that her feelings for her mother be sound and that she should unconsciously pattern herself on the female parent. Girls who do not go through this normal emotional evolution often have great trouble later in their sexual identity. In Jacqueline's case, she had as an example a most admirable mother. That Janet Bouvier's grace and breeding communicated themselves to the small girl is evident in Jackie's behavior in later years, when her hospitality, warmth, taste and charm became such tremendous assets in the White House. A mother does not educate by words alone. Jacqueline's mother has remarked to friends that she never tried to tell her daughter what to do. Yet by her own attitudes, she set a high standard for her daughter to emulate.

Not that Jackie was by any means a tractable child. A series of nurses and governesses found her a handful. She was a bundle of endless curiosity, which found direction in animals, books and her adored father. Because her mother taught her early to ride, she spent more time with her mother than do most children in her social milieu. During this period, there was the first evidence of the child's fantastic memory that was to be both a trial and an asset during her debutante days. When she had raced through *Peter Rabbit, Little Lord Fauntleroy* and the assembly-line new additions to the *Little Colonel* books, she turned to the adult fiction in the guest room.

During her fifth year, Jackie had developed enough poise and skill to ride on a hunter beside her mother. That summer, mother and daughter, mounted on chestnut mares, won third prize in the Family Class at the East Hampton Horse Show.

The little girl had inherited also her mother's love for animals. Mrs. Bouvier's horses were adored by all members of the family. They were the family pets, lovingly cared for.

Jackie was aware early in her youth of the importance of impeccable riding clothes. Her mother's riding habits invariably aroused applause in even the hardened sports writers. One fashion authority wrote of Mrs. Bouvier: ". . . she wears the very smartest in riding habits at Long Island horse shows. She's shown here in complete costume: top hat, ascot tie, coat with contrasting collar and trousers to match the collar. Long leather boots, of course. . . ."

In the photographs of Jacqueline of that period, we see a

small girl in jodhpurs and jacket, shirt open at the throat, and a felt soft hat pulled down over her forehead.

Whenever Jackie took the applause of the crowd too seriously, after she had shown courage and sportsmanship in taking a spill and trying to remount her pony, her mother lectured her sternly on her duty toward her mount.

Jackie's father did not participate actively in the horse shows from Saratoga and Churchill Downs and Aiken. But he was usually an interested spectator, and his small daughter was often behind him. A reporter called her Long Island's youngest horse-show fan, and made a comment that is worth marking. He said, although she was "too young now to rival her mother's feats in the equine world, the promising young rider has been a spectator at every important contest for several seasons."

The following summer, Jackie was a winner at the Southhampton Horse Show for Children Under Nine. She rode regularly, profiting by her mother's guidance, and at the age of eleven she won two outstanding prizes for horsemanship.

Until that year, the only cloud on the childish horizon had been the birth of her sister, Lee. Jackie, three at that time, had been the little adored despot of the family. In spite of her independence and obstinacy, she was a gay, merry child whom adults found irresistible.

No doubt for these reasons she may have suffered the pangs of sibling rivalry more acutely perhaps than the children who arrived on an annual basis in the Joseph Kennedy family. It is difficult for a little princess to share the throne, and at three, when the child's emotions are on a selfish primitive level, it requires the greatest parental tact and understanding to help the youngster make the adjustment.

After baby Lee's birth, in the spring of 1933, Jacqueline was given her own bedroom. It was filled with her stuffed animals, books and the rag doll Sammy, her regular bedfellow.

The difference in the sisters' appearance was marked.

Lee is very small, like her mother, with a delicate, pointed face that reflects her feelings. She is gentle, soft-spoken, extremely tactful and sensitive to the feelings of others.

Jackie often puts honesty before diplomacy. In spite of her soft small-girl voice, she can be passionately emphatic. During their early years, the sisters were dressed alike by their mother, who approved of simple classic garments for young people.

But Lee, in spite of her modesty, always was partial to vivid, high-fashion garments. Jackie, on the other hand, preferred the more acceptable muted tones, although she has always had a passion for all shades of pink.

There was a silent, unacknowledged rivalry between the two sisters that simmered but seldom boiled over. What brought them finally together and united them in a single entity against the world was the tragic event that shattered their tranquil lives during the year when Jackie turned eleven and Lee eight.

The gay, charming young Bouviers separated.

Janet Bouvier asked for a divorce. There was a hint of scandal, of another woman, and since the only grounds for divorce in New York State is adultery, this may have been probable.

As much as the girls were shielded from the facts, reality nevertheless intruded in their lives. From backstairs gossip they no doubt heard that their mother had charged their father with misconduct, which he was to deny.

But they already knew their parents were about to establish different residences, for both father and mother had told them, with admirable restraint that did not entirely mask their sorrow, of their plans to separate.

It took six months before the lawyers worked out a property settlement and arrangements for the custody of the girls. Then Janet Bouvier went to Nevada for the divorce. Since divorce is a simple process in that state, the entire family was saved from further humiliating revelations that might make newspaper headlines.

Before that, however, mother and daughters moved from the Park Avenue duplex to a smaller apartment at One Gracie Square.

"Visitation privileges" is a phrase Jacqueline had cause to loathe, for it meant that no longer would she see her adored father each day. It meant marking time six days in order to spend the seventh with him. It meant sharing with him only one half of each school vacation and six weeks in the summer. Is there any child who doesn't weep inwardly at the injustice of being torn between two beloved parents, having not enough of either one of them?

The Bouviers were rich, Republican Catholics, and divorce was a simpler technical process for them than it might be for less affluent parishioners.

Nevertheless, the effect of the separation was no less painful for their children. Although their mother was Episcopalian, Jacqueline and her sister received normal training as dutiful Catholics; they were baptized and confirmed. But in the family milieu, there was less of the emphasis on religion and more on the cosmopolitan sporting and social life. It is doubtful if during those days the two sisters, suddenly thrown on themselves, found sustenance in the bosom of the Church. If anyone shared Jacqueline's private grief, it was her animals.

During this ordeal, there is no doubt that Janet Bouvier, with all the sensitivity and love she lavished on her children and her horses, dedicated herself to making the loss of a father more bearable to her daughters. Certainly she was aware of the danger of emotional damage to the girls, particularly the older one. A world suddenly divided becomes a puzzling, hostile world to a child who has been nourished in the cocoon of united parental affection.

Nor could this have been an easy time for Janet Bouvier. No matter how divergent are the personalities of husband and wife, which consequently become the cause of a split, a young woman is apt to blame herself for the schism. Perhaps in the dark lonely hours of the night, Janet Bouvier chided herself for being so self-contained, so aware of breeding and proper behavior—virtues that may have served as a dampening influence on a man of her husband's vitality and enthusiasms.

Whatever she told her daughters, after the initial announcements, has remained in the privacy of their hearts. No evidence of anything but an impeccable wall of defense was noted by family or friends.

Yet for Jacqueline, particularly, it was a time of suffering that arrived at a crucial moment in her development. She was going into the teens, when adolescence takes its toll of body and personality, when the maturation of sex glands, the shaping of character are buffeted by the whims and inconsistencies of a confused lingering childhood.

A girl's father is her first love. His behavior toward her usually determines her future reaction to the men in her life. If her father has encouraged her to feel feminine, if he has awarded her unconditional love, she will approach marriage with confidence and trust. None of the horrors of fear or anger will burden her conscience. She will accept her own husband with an eager, unquestioning and loving heart. She will without a feeling of sacrifice put his happiness first.

We hear again and again, from a multitude of sources, that her father was the most important person in Jacqueline's life.

Often, after a divorce, young girls unconsciously blame the mother for the tragedy. Perhaps they think: *It is your fault. If you were more of a woman, he would not have left us*. Whether this thought ever came to the surface of Jacqueline's mind isn't shown, of course. But what is known is that her relationship with her mother has always been warm and good.

Nevertheless, this was the beginning of Jackie's tendency to withdraw into her private world. She learned to participate and yet remain an onlooker. It was perhaps a saving grace, enabling her to face what was unspeakably painful.

There was to be evidence of her ability to tune out during her years as wife of a young Senator and later the President. Often, at formal dinners, those near her were aware of the fact that while her smile was warm, her manner attentive, she seemed to be in a place where they dared not intrude.

As a child she had always been sturdy, stocky, with a beautiful head somewhat out of proportion for her build. Now there was the kind of plumpness that is not only baby fat but accompanies a child's deep inner emotional needs.

The bright, confident energetic little girl changed. She grew shy. To hide her shyness, she adopted a rather aloof and regal manner that irritated her young friends. Adolescence wrought loneliness, a need for inner retreat and a search for self without satisfaction.

She developed a private core that no one has since touched.

Adolescent girls can be cruel and sadistic, and her friends turned on Jacqueline. Misinterpreting her behavior, they called her "Jacqueline Borgia."

If these cutting remarks sent her deeper into her shell, they also indirectly contributed to her budding future. Isolation is not as unhealthy as one would think. A certain amount of isolation is a requisite to growth. Some of our most talented people have suffered in adolescence from an acute sense of loneliness.

Her days passed in a dreamlike trance. She went through all the gestures expected of her at school, but most of her life was an inner one. Once she mentioned to a friend that it might be fun to grow up to be a circus queen and marry the man on the flying trapeze.

Although this was a girlish, flippant remark, it is revealing. For the circus, all tinsel and gaiety, abounding with glamor and feats of skill and daring, is often the end of the rainbow for many young people who cannot make peace with their present lives. It has a special lure for children who chafe at restraint, convention and conformity. And the flying surely in some way appealed to her as a departure from the confining world of the rich little schoolgirl.

For Jacqueline, the week held one day—Sunday.

With each day of separation, her need and adoration of her father grew in intensity. There has always been an unflagging drive to her emotions. For all the detached manner, she is evidently a cauldron of deep feelings.

Fortunately, Jack Bouvier's awareness of her dark moods took a constructive form. He loved his daughters too much to allow them to suffer for the flaws in his personal life. His imagination and sense of good fun did much to restore Jacqueline's equanimity. To have a father as handsome as Black Jack Bouvier, as universally admired, as athletic and fun-loving was a monumental asset to a growing girl. Especially a father who made her feel so special. Just as Jacqueline acquired her love of history from her grandfather, John Bouvier, she shared with his son—her own father—a love of all sorts of living creatures.

When she was living with her mother and sister in a smaller Gracie Square apartment, the first year of her parents' separation, her father often arranged with a pet store to lease an animal for their Sunday jaunt—preferably a mongrel whose blue blood wasn't nearly as important as his need for love. Accompanied by the little fellow, father and daughter would take off at a healthy clip for Central Park.

Other Sundays, he took Jacqueline and her friends to lunch at Schrafft's and to the movies. This was usually followed by an ice-cream binge, and he never criticized the rich whipped-cream concoctions, although her nurse often complained that Jackie's appetite for supper was ruined. Jack Bouvier had an elemental earthy enjoyment of life which communicated itself to everyone who came in contact with him. It was as if the earth itself lived within his physical senses.

Yet being so manly, he was not ashamed to reveal the tender side of his nature.

When his young daughters suddenly realized that vivisection was practiced on animals, their anguish knew no bounds. It was he who helped them draft telegrams of protest to the New York *Journal-American.*

Occasionally he drove Jacqueline out to Belmont Park, where his friends included the foremost jockeys of their day. These were precious moments that she could not share with her sister, Lee.

Yet, in a way, their parents' divorce was instrumental in bringing the two sisters into harmony. Perhaps the need for each other overcame the initial obstacles of sibling rivalry. For now they stood together with pride and solidarity. With their mother, they suffered through the period of mourning that, whether through divorce or death, must be lived through in order to step back again into life.

Jacqueline continued to see her father often until his death in 1957. To her great joy, he and her husband became friends, for they had much in common. Perhaps, that dreadful day after her husband's death, when she murmured something to the effect that his shining light was no more, she was referring not only to him but to the first man in her life.

From the beginning, studies came easily to Jacqueline. In spite of her whims and her independence which bordered on obstinacy, she showed early a gift for life.

Her mother, now Mrs. Hugh Auchincloss, has said, "I like to use the world 'original' in describing Jacqueline. She was brilliant, with strong feelings about things, gifted artistically and always good in her studies."

It is interesting to note that her grandfather, John Vernou Bouvier, Jr., was an intellectual genius. At sixteen, he enrolled at Columbia University and graduated at twenty with a B.A. degree and a Phi Beta Kappa key, a prize for winning the Chanler Historical Essay, and triple collegiate awards as Honor Man, valedictorian, and vice president of the class of 1886. He was an authority on the United States Constitution, and no doubt would have been happily impressed with his grandson-in-law, John F. Kennedy.

Jacqueline spent a year at Miss Yates's preschool nursery. From there, she entered Miss Chapin's School, a private institution where little girls of wealth and cultured background were taught, in addition to their usual studies, the art of becoming ladies.

There was a singularly democratic atmosphere at the school. Students wore blue linen uniforms and were challenged to put the best efforts into their work.

Miss Ethel Stringfellow, the headmistress, was a woman of enlightenment and good sense. Her aim was to teach her girls that life takes adjusting to, and that the most effective means toward achieving that goal are courtesy, self-discipline and hard work. To be summoned to Miss Stringfellow's office for an infraction of rules was a source of fear and humiliation for most girls. Jacqueline, however, seemed to glory in it. It was one of her first ventures in rebellion.

Already quick-witted and precocious, she found school much too easy. Because of this most of her energies exploded into mischief. She was a sore trial to the headmistress. Mothers of her little friends commented that she was "the very worst girl in school."

None of Miss Stringfellow's lectures made the slightest dent on her young pupil. As a last desperate resort, the headmistress appealed to Jacqueline's passion for horses. She told the girl that even a thoroughbred, if not disciplined, is destined for failure.

This was the moment of truth. Here was a comparison that not only made sense to Jacqueline but appealed to her more constructive instincts.

She changed from rebel to leader.

Years later, she said that Miss Stringfellow was the "first great moral influence" in her life.

No doubt, the transformation in her young daughter's behavior was something of a miracle to the harassed Janet Bouvier.

It was especially gratifying for her to hear the headmistress ruefully explain, "I mightn't have kept Jacqueline, except that she has the most inquiring mind we'd had in the school in thirty-five years."

During her student days at Miss Chapin's and later at Miss Porter's, Jackie's love of reading and the turbulence of her inner feelings resulted in a flood of spontaneous poems. One of them was more memorable for the delicate and lovely sketches that surrounded the paper on which it was printed than for the verse itself. But the words already verify the private mystical needs in her nature.

This poem first appeared in Mary Van Rensselaer Thayer's biography of Jacqueline.

Sea Joy

When I go down by the sandy shore
I can think of nothing I want more
Than to live by the booming blue sea
As the seagulls flutter about me.
I can run about when the tide is out
With the wind and the sand and the sea all about
And the seagulls are swirling and diving for fish
Oh—to live by the sea is my only wish.

Me—1939

And another, which holds an even truer key to her youthful dreams.

I love walking on the shore
To watch the angry sea,
Where summer people were before
And now there's only me. . . .

The pull of the sea and the lonely dunes is one of the links that forged the chain of love for Jacqueline and her husband, John Kennedy. Photographer Mark Shaw took the photograph that was reputed to be the President's favorite. This is a picture of John F. Kennedy, in jersey shirt and slacks, his jacket carelessly hunched under his arm, walking along the sand dunes near Hyannis Port. There is the vast brooding sweep of sky above him, the dunes and the wildflowers and berries encroaching on the sand, and although the figure of the President is small in the framework, there is a suggestion of lonely grandeur, of communication between man and spirit that is ineffably moving.

That she was a romantic is evident by her choice of books. At eleven, she had read *Gone With the Wind* no less than three times. In her early teens, her literary taste ran to Lord Byron, whose colorful life story and whose poems she knew almost by heart.

The development of her artistic and intellectual interests continued throughout Jacqueline's growing years. She adored the ballet; wrote little stories and poems. She was no doubt greatly encouraged in her pursuit of self-expression by her devoted Bouvier grandfather, who himself had written a poem to celebrate each of her birthdays. She much preferred Miss O'Neill's ballet classes to Mrs. Hubbell's lessons in ballroom dancing and deportment. Her collection of ballet books was large. Although she came to realize that perhaps her height of five feet seven inches would keep her from being a successful ballerina, she did at one time consider a career in theatrical and ballet costume design. She already showed at an early age much promise as a primitive artist.

Looking back at her adolescence, Jacqueline feels the most thrilling moment came when her father took her to the gallery of the New York Stock Exchange.

Today, she recalls with gratitude that her father and her husband did get to know and respect each other. There was never any rivalry for her affection between the two men she so deeply loved.

Jacqueline was a rather plump adolescent, still divided between moments of elation and periods of shy withdrawal when she entered Miss Porter's School in Farmington, Connecticut.

This new period of adjustment appears to have aroused a fresh storm of rebellion within her. When her turn came to wait on tables, she managed artfully to spill a creamy pie in a teacher's lap. She had a singular talent for foraging for sweets in a kitchen that was off limits for the students. Her roommate at that time was Nancy Tuckerman, whom she later brought to the White House as her social secretary.

Since for her, life was incomplete without an animal to love and care for, she longed passionately to have one of her mother's horses stabled at the school. Many of Miss Porter's girls had generous allowances which enabled them to board their horses there. But her mother was impervious to her appeal, so Jacqueline turned to her Grandfather Bouvier for help. He came across with the munificent sum of twenty-five dollars a month, and Mrs. Bouvier allowed her daughter the loan of her own beloved mare, Danseuse. Thus, the presence of the mare and the funds to board her combined to make Jacqueline a more happy and relaxed student.

It was inevitable that her love for animals should translate itself into children's stories. Family pets, family anniversaries, holidays were usually marked by stories or poems written by Jacqueline, and her audience was no less appreciative than the country itself was to be a couple of decades later.

During the period when her teachers considered her a beautiful and gifted youngster, she was also the tomboy of East Hampton. It was a matter of pride with her to keep up with her regiment of boy cousins, mostly Bouviers. Her favorite was Scotty, the son of one of her aunts. He was, she decided, an extremely naughty boy, a fact which aroused tremendous admiration within her. During those rough-and-tumble play periods, her wild unruly hair was disciplined into thick braids and her sturdy body was clad in sensible togs. In spite of her quick temper and her tendency to throw tantrums, she was considered a good sport, and she aroused the adoration of the younger children, including her sister, Lee.

She was almost compulsive in her need for perfection. All of her actions during this growing period were quick, impatient and dynamic. Whenever she got too difficult, her Grandmother Bouvier had the pat answer for her behavior.

Mary Van Rensselaer Thayer reports it deadpan in Jacqueline's biography. The elderly Mrs. Bouvier would say, "Why, that's only Jackie's French temperament showing."

Much of Jacqueline's volatile temperament went into exile, however, in June, 1942.

That was when Janet Bouvier took her second husband.

She became the wife of the twice-married Hugh D. Auchincloss.

Hugh Auchincloss came of Scottish ancestry. He was born in Newport, attended Yale and Columbia Law School, and practiced law in New York before opening his own brokerage firm in Washington. He was kind and steadfast, admirable qualities for a woman to enjoy in a durable relationship. In later years, Jacqueline said warmly, "He was a wonderful stepfather."

The acquisition of her stepfather, whom she always called "Uncle Hugh," brought Jacqueline into a new atmosphere of additional relatives by marriage.

The homes were the Auchincloss estate in Virginia, called Merrywood, a sprawling house of many bedrooms and ample attractions for a young brood—a swimming pool, badminton court, stables, surrounded by forty-six acres of secluded grounds; and the spacious, old-fashioned, rambling house in Newport, called Hammersmith Farm. This estate, which Hugh Auchincloss inherited from his parents, was originally a productive working farm. But in recent years the place has become a comfortable summer retreat for the Auchincloss family. Although the house was casually furnished, Jacqueline's artistic taste encouraged a certain decorative unity. Since the downstairs walls were white, the carpeting red, her suggestion was that all dogs the family planned to acquire should be black. As a result, the house was generously populated with tanned children and anthracite black poodles, Scotties and cocker spaniels.

Now there were five children—Jacqueline and Lee, and Hugh's children by previous marriages. These were Hugh, Jr., who was known affectionately as Yusha; and Nina and Tommy. During the ensuing years, two children were born to Janet and Hugh: a lovely girl, Janet, who greatly resembled her older half-sister, Jacqueline; and a boy, Jamie.

No doubt all children managed to live in the turbulent harmony of the young in the spacious winter estate and summer farm. But with such a variety of temperaments, there was perhaps a good deal of fireworks. But it was no doubt snuffed out quickly by the good manners expected of the children and the loving determination of the parents to weld them into a warm affectionate family.

Jacqueline, of course, remained passionately loyal to her own father. Her mother had been meticulously fair in making sure no word of criticism ever touched Black Jack Bouvier in his daughter's presence, nor did she discourage her child's emotional ties to her father. However, with all the warmth, tact and understanding at her command, she created a climate of adjustment that made life serene for her two girls.

Jacqueline continued to keep in touch with her father; her adoration did not diminish. As a matter of fact, in future years, it became the obsessive spark in her life. His visits to her school were always a highlight, and she needed out of pride and overflowing joy to share him with her schoolmates.

"All my friends adored him and used to line up to be taken out to dinner when he came to see me," she has said. "He'd take batches of us out to the Elm Tree Inn. Everybody ordered steaks and two desserts. We must have eaten him broke. He was a most devastating figure. . . ."

Two beautiful homes, her beloved animals, a growing devotion to, and understanding with, her sister, Lee, nevertheless did not ease the inner anguish of Jacqueline's emotional struggle toward maturity.

During the stormy adolescent years, she was thrust from a two-child home, snug as a mink-lined womb, into a world in which she had to share her mother with a man and children who were strangers to her.

The vexing problems of the normal family constellation are simple compared to the complexities that arise in a mixed household. With stepchildren coming from both the new mother and the new father, and finally children of their own union, there are bound to be tensions and conflicts.

The fact that the new menage is luxurious, with no financial or social insecurities, does not ease the emotional burden of children of divorce.

Seldom do parents analyze the dangers of such relationships, for they are apt to be raw and painful, and good manners demand that one skirts any embarrassing situation.

But ignoring facts does not screen out the children's reactions. Here is a new figure to take the place of the adored father. No matter how thoughtful and considerate he may be, he is, for the child, a symbol of the usurper. Yet his very tenderness, humor and consideration may leave a child also with a pervading sense of guilt that results in unwarranted gusts of inner uncontrollable fury.

In a scholarly inquiry called *Life, Stress and Mental Health*, the writers come to the general conclusion that remarriage "often fails as far as the mental health of the stepchildren is concerned."

For it is often easier for a child to accept the death of a father than to reconcile herself to a substitute. It becomes particularly difficult when the real father is in the background and is himself a charming, affectionate human being who exerts a tremendous magnetism on his young daughters.

This puts the stepfather on the spot. No matter how fine he is, how noble his intentions, he is nearly always licked before the start. In his sincere desire to fulfill his obligation to his new stepchildren, he is apt to err on the side of the angels. Terrified of being branded callous or unkind, he overcompensates with generosity and indulgence. He shies away from disciplining his new brood. Yet discipline is what they expect from him, and his very forbearance adds to their feeling of being outsiders.

Suggestions that Jacqueline might have accepted joyously from her own father may have caused her pain coming from Uncle Hugh. During this period, her aloofness toward her younger sister, Lee, who was so filled with admiration and worship, melted. The two became inseparable. It was as though, in their union, they found added strength to defy the world.

When the first child is born of a new alliance, children of the first marriage often consider the infant a supplanter. The birth tends to emphasize the loss of their own father. As a result, they transform the inner guilt feelings of which they are blissfully unaware into a torrent of love for the new arrival.

In a mixed household, we have "her" children and "his" children and "their" children, and often the gay warm togetherness is only surface smooth.

It seems probable that Uncle Hugh encouraged the girls' reverence for their own father. And by patience, kindness and a slow Scottish humor, he won them over. Jackie discovered in him what each child so desperately wants in a step parent—a good friend.

A frequent visitor to the family circle was Gore Vidal, later to become a best-selling novelist and playwright. He was to write *The Best Man,* a primer on American politics for Broadway.

Vidal was to campaign on the Kennedy platform in 1960, but the playwright's efforts to win a congressional seat in New York's 29th District, embracing five counties in the mid-Hudson Valley, met with failure.

Vidal shared Jacqueline's stepfather. Uncle Hugh had once been married to his mother, Nina Oldes Vidal.

Jacqueline spent two years at Holton-Arms, a Washington private day school. Her favorite teacher was Miss Helen Shear, in spite of the fact that she was the Latin instructor. Jacqueline had from childhood been encouraged in her pursuit of French. It was an asset that would serve her well in the future. When the family gave French-speaking luncheons, however, Jacqueline mischievously switched to German. At Holton-Arms, she took Spanish also, and even today her bookshelves are filled with records of conversational French and Spanish.

At Farmington, where she was sent at fifteen, she managed her studies nicely. She averaged A-minus, and yet the headmaster, Ward L. Johnson, wrote on her report card, "Jacqueline could do better." He no doubt sensed her fantastic potential; nevertheless, his comments were a source of displeasure to Mrs. Auchincloss.

During her first term at Miss Porter's, Jacqueline received letters from her beloved Grandfather Bouvier that stressed the code of behavior and did much to influence her later tendency to modesty and the kind of good manners that spring from a thoughtful heart.

According to Mary Van Rensselaer Thayer, he wrote her in part:

> The capacity to adapt oneself to his or her environment not only marks evolutionary progress, but discloses a practical philosophy which it is more wise to cultivate.
>
> With you, happily, this process of adaptation has not been in the remotest degree difficult. You enjoy Farmington and all the things it has to offer, the most important among which is the adequate preparation for future feats of work and responsibility. . . . I discern in you more than passing evidence of leadership, but before leading others, we must guide and direct ourselves. This is the true way to usefulness in life. . . . You will observe that those who are useful are the best contributors to the correct leading of life and in the last analysis are the most efficient and most contented members of all God's creatures. But don't be pretentious or labor under the false impression of indispensability. To do so spells the prig, either male or female. . . .

Whatever deep spiritual quality was sleeping in Jacqueline's private self was surely coaxed into being by her grandfather's sagacious counseling.

Jacqueline was fifteen when her half sister, Janet Jennings Auchincloss, was born. In a gay poem written to her mother, Jacqueline prophesied that Janet Jennings would enter politics at twenty-one and become the first woman President.

Young Janet, who is now a post-debutante herself, shows no inclination for the political arena, but Jacqueline's poem surely had a touch of prescience.

Jamie, the last of the Auchincloss clan, was born just before Jacqueline's graduation from Miss Porter's. During this period, the deep glowing love Jacqueline gave her horses and dogs was shared by her half sister and half brother. She spent endless hours writing and illustrating children's stories for them. Her capacity for touching children at their own level, her own uncomplicated love for the young and innocent of heart, gave the children a rare experience in sisterly attention. Later, this gift was to be the fount from which she drew in her devotion toward her own children, Caroline and John.

At five months, Jamie shared a special party with his half sister. He was christened the same afternoon his parents gave a tea to introduce Jacqueline to society. The invitation read:

TO MEET

MISS JACQUELINE LEE BOUVIER

AND

MASTER JAMES LEE AUCHINCLOSS

In Miss Porter's yearbook for the class of 1947, there is this revealing profile of Jacqueline:

Jacqueline Lee Bouvier
"Merrywood"
McLean, Virginia
"Jackie"
Favorite Song: "Lime House Blues"
Always Saying: "Play a Rumba next."
Best Known For: Wit
Aversion: People who ask if her horse
is still alive.
Where Found: Laughing with Tucky.
Ambition: Not to be a housewife.

Chapter Three

The summer before she was to enter Vassar, Jacqueline was honored by her mother and stepfather with a dinner dance at Newport's venerable Clambake Club.

The affair turned out to be one of the most lavish balls of the season. Jacqueline and Rose Grosvenor, the debutante daughter of the Theodore Grosvenors, shared honors. The Clambake Club is open to the ladies only on rare occasions, at which time they are graciously allowed to partake of the superb clam chowder, lobsters and deep-dish apple pie for which the club is famous.

For the dinner dance, the club rooms were draped in fresh-scented flowers from the gardens of both debutantes. Blue lights winked like sapphires on the terrace.

Mrs. Auchincloss, still recuperating from the birth of her infant son, lacked the strength to go shopping for the bright occasion with her eldest daughter. Jacqueline was allowed to choose her own gown. Although her mother primed her to shop with an eye for expensive glamor, Jacqueline bought a dress off the rack in a New York department store. It was not precisely what her elegant mother would have chosen. But with Jacqueline's dark glossy hair, her unusually beautiful and distinctive features and her body grown willowy, the simple tulle gown with its bouffant skirt was enchantingly effective.

That Jackie was the star of the ball was self-evident. Yet, before the evening was over, her quiet fourteen-year-old kid sister, Lee, managed to steal a good bit of the spotlight for herself.

Mrs. Auchincloss, who never allowed herself to deviate from classic good taste, had chosen a suitable teen-age frock for Lee. But the youngster had her own ideas of what to wear at her sister's debut.

How much of her decision stemmed from admiration, how much from pure mischief, how much from an unconscious desire to compete with the adored older sister, were never acknowledged by the mischievous miss. But she did make a breathtaking entrance. Clad in a strapless pink satin, which glittered with a rash of rhinestones, with fingerless black satin gloves, the young imp resembled nothing less than a juvenile Hollywood starlet. Debutantes of the evening in faultless pristine white watched helplessly as the baby vamp devastated the stag line.

Mrs. Auchincloss' reactions to Lee's improvisation were laced with amusement. Even Jacqueline finally saw humor in it. At any rate, she borrowed Lee's pink satin for later parties. Perhaps her admitted passion for the color pink stemmed from this incident.

Jacqueline cut a dashing and romantic figure as a debutante. Igor Cassini, who as Cholly Knickerbocker was the social arbiter of the *Journal-American,* nominated her the Debutante of the Year, a natural successor to the fabulous Brenda Frazier.

He wrote:

> America is a country of traditions. Every four years we elect a President, every two years our Congressmen. And every year a new Queen of Debutantes is crowned . . . Queen Deb of the Year is Jacqueline Bouvier, a regal brunette who has classic features and the daintiness of Dresden porcelain. She has poise, is soft-spoken and intelligent, everything the leading debutante should be. Her background is strictly "Old Guard." . . . Jacqueline is now studying at Vassar. . . .

Although a goodly number of socialites chose Vassar for its social status, the college takes its curriculum seriously. Girls are expected to allocate ample time for study, and social service to one's future community is stressed.

Jacqueline's college boards were exceptionally high—she had a 90 percentile rating—and she decided on Vassar because it was the chosen college of so many of her friends.

If college was a disappointment to her, she put the blame on herself. While most girls were taken with extracurricular benefits—weekends in New York for parties or weekends at the Ivy League colleges—Jacqueline soon discovered that the life of a typical college freshman afforded her little satisfaction.

A few discerning friends realized her personality was reaching out for new frontiers; that what she had absorbed over the adolescent years was maturing and shaping her personality. Since it was her time of transition, she found it amusing to date often and a variety of young men. Indeed, her admirers were too abundant, so that her father suggested whimsically he would soon lose her to some "funny-looking gink." However, he added on a more serious note, "Perhaps you'll use your head and wait until you are at least twenty-one."

He need not have been concerned. Jacqueline was evidently unsure of her emotions. As a result, she kept her dates on a cool and casual basis. Often she knew more about sports than the young men who accompanied her to football games or tennis matches. Yet she managed to establish a wide-eyed Lorelei Lee aura because she felt it was expected of her. The tragedy that often besets clever young girls like Jacqueline in that they are cautioned from childhood never to reveal to their escorts the depth of their minds. This no doubt contributes to their affinity for men older than themselves.

According to a report in *Time* Magazine, which featured a radiantly beautiful portrait of her on the cover, a young socialite who had dated Jacqueline during her Vassar period said she had the reputation of being very frigid.

"She was rather aloof and reserved," he added, "but everybody liked her, although she seemed to talk an awful lot about animals."

At Vassar, she dressed in the classic uniform of the well-bred Eastern college girl: good woolens—fine fabrics have always interested her—simple sweaters, skirts, and understated dresses. In describing her appearance, a fellow student says, "We were wearing our hair in deep waves falling to the shoulders. It didn't really suit Jackie. Today she has acquired much more of an international, cosmopolitan look."

In spite of her inner quest for direction, Jacqueline managed to absorb an ample amount of intellectual nourishment in her first two years at Vassar. She found Helen Sandison's Shakespearean lectures stimulating, and Florence Lovell's course on the history of religion intriguing.

Little has been written about Jacqueline's religious feelings during these growing years. She was brought up as a Catholic. Yet the formal side of her religion seems to have played less of a role than her awareness of life around her, her reverent love for nature and animals, which was in itself the simplest and most touching form of religion. A young girl who was finding dissatisfaction with the background of her life would inevitably begin to probe at the deepening meanings of her life, and this would surely lead her into a search for a more meaningful form of faith. She was yet to find it in the formal teachings of her church.

Her first year at Vassar completed, Jacqueline visited Europe for the first time, in the company of three other girls —Julia Bissell and Helen and Judy Bowdoin, stepdaughters of the then Under-Secretary of the Treasury, Edward F. Foley, Jr. They were chaperoned by Miss Helen Shearman, who had taught Jacqueline Latin at the Holton-Arms School. The highlight of the trip was an invitation to a Royal Garden Party at Buckingham Palace. The girls were decked out in handsome afternoon frocks, wide-brimmed straw hats and elbow-length gloves. They were much too excited to mind the rain that ruined the afternoon perfection. They went down the receiving line twice, and although they were not formally presented to the late George VI and the Queen, they did have the thrill of shaking hands with Sir Winston Churchill.

A tour of France including a brief but exhilarating stay in Paris followed. They continued on to Switzerland and Italy, and finally, their heads filled with a kaleidoscope of brilliant scenes, returned reluctantly home.

As gifts—for the family butler who had a weakness for horseflesh, Jacqueline brought back an English racing form; for a religious maid, a rosary blessed by the Pope.

What she had seen of France made her eager to explore that country in greater detail. Although she was studying at Vassar, she heard that Smith arranged for their college girls to spend their junior year abroad. She immediately set wheels working to enable her to share in a similar privilege.

Late that summer of 1949, Jacqueline, fortified by her parents' blessings, returned to France, to study first at the University of Grenoble and then at the Sorbonne.

While at the University of Grenoble, Jacqueline lived with a French family. This gave her a stimulating opportunity to refine her accent and to get an insight into her forebears' way of life. She found an immediate affinity for the people. French students in her classes were wonderfully generous about helping her with her compositions. The lovely verdant countryside with its rows of tall poplars aroused a romantic response in her. She wrote her family descriptions of the inhabitants and the land with poetic perception that made her letters a treasure to her doting relatives.

At the Sorbonne, she studied French civilization and literature. Most of the American college girls lived at Reid Hall, a dorm for American students. But Jacqueline preferred to board with a French family. She moved into the apartment of Comtesse de Renty, a charming impoverished French woman whose husband has last been heard of in a German concentration camp.

The Comtesse had also been imprisoned during World War II. Now she was reduced to opening her home to paying guests. She was a woman of courage, utterly lacking in self-pity; she shopped and cooked for her menage of seven with Gallic humor and equanimity.

Unfortunately, the apartment was unheated; Paris was suffering from a shortage of coal. Jacqueline often studied swathed in an outfit that suggested a trip to the Swiss Alps.

Yet physical discomforts, such as the use of sweaters, caps and mittens as usual indoor outfits, did not unduly bother Jacqueline. As a matter of fact, she seemed rather to enjoy it, since it was her first introduction to physical discomforts. Moreover, the admirable character traits of the Comtesse made a permanent impression on the young girl. The older woman, having survived terror and the threat of death, was able nonetheless to face life with a certain élan. It was a unique gift called style, and Jacqueline was unconsciously to make it a part of herself.

When her mother and her Uncle Hugh paid her a visit in Paris, they were delighted with her display of discipline and fortitude. With Claude de Renty, daughter of the Comtesse, Jacqueline took a vacation through Germany and Austria. Since they traveled third class, it was an experience that again opened a new world to the young Bouvier—the world of the average middle-class family had previously been unfamiliar to her.

Her French was perfected in the home of the Comtesse, for there English was never spoken. And her love for Paris grew into a lovely obsession.

On her return to the United States, Jacqueline was reluctant to return to Vassar. Instead, she remained in Washington, close to her family, and majored in art at George Washington University. Both her family and friends were aware of the deep change in her. The year in France had performed the miracle. From a restless questing girl, she had developed into a mature, thoughtful young woman, less shy, more poised and more confident of her goals.

At her mother's suggestion, Jacqueline decided to enter a contest sponsored by *Vogue*. The annual Prix de Paris offers the winner a six-months' stint on Paris *Vogue* and equal time in the New York offices. To win it is a tremendous step forward for any girl interested in a fashion career. That year, the contest attracted entries from 1,280 aspirants.

The applicants had no easy job cut out for them. Qualifications entailed the submission of a plan for an entire issue of *Vogue;* four technical papers dealing with high fashion, and an essay on "People I Wish I Had Known."

Jacqueline's choice of the personality reveals an interesting facet of her own character. The men who intrigued her were Charles Baudelaire, the effete French poet; Oscar Wilde, the brilliant Irish-English author; and Sergei Diaghilev, the Russian impresario of the ballet.

In charming literate prose, she suggests that Baudelaire and Wilde "both were poets and idealists who could paint sinfulness with honesty and still believe in something higher."

Her admiration for Wilde centered on his wit and epigrams, a talent she was later to discover and enjoy in her own husband.

She admired Sergei Diaghilev for his ability to coordinate a superb production—the music of Rimsky-Korsakov, the backgrounds of Bakst, the choreography of Fokine and the dancing of Nijinsky. In the White House, in a future period, she was to find herself in the position of an amateur impresario, blending her exquisite state dinners with entertainment by the greatest artists of her country's culture.

It may be enlightening to quote from the epigrams of Wilde that perhaps had stimulated her vivid imagination.

> Anyone can sympathize with the suffering of a friend, but it requires a very fine nature to sympathize with a friend's success.
>
> A man who desires to get married should know either everything or nothing.
>
> All charming people are spoiled. It is the secret of their attraction.

> The only difference between the saint and the sinner is that every saint has a past and every sinner has a future.
>
> It is through art, and through art only, that we can realize our perfection; through art and through art only, that we can shield ourselves from the sordid perils of actual existence.
>
> The best way to make children good is to make them happy.

And Charles Baudelaire, who said of the battle between the sexes:

> He gets on best with women who best knows how to get on without them. A sweetheart is a bottle of wine; a woman is a wine bottle.
>
> Woman's courage is ignorance of danger; man's is hope of escape.

One should suspect that the writings of these worldly sophisticated men had a good deal of influence on Jacqueline's inquisitive mind. For she seemed to have absorbed fresh ideas like an avid sponge.

That she was awarded first prize in the contest was inevitable. The judges were particularly taken with her choice of the people she had wished to have known.

Nevertheless, in deference to her family's wishes, she didn't accept the award. Although they were justifiably proud of her achievement, her mother and Uncle Hugh felt that she had spent enough time away from home and should be close to her family hearth for a while.

Jacqueline was agreeable to their suggestions. She admitted at a later time, "I guess I was scared to go. I felt then that if I went back I'd live there forever, because I loved Paris so much. . . ."

So she traveled instead in 1950 to Ireland, with her stepbrother, Yusha. On a second trip, she was accompanied by her sister, Lee. They celebrated Jacqueline's twenty-second birthday in Florence, where their meanderings through the countryside were highlighted by a visit to the late art authority, Bernard Berenson, who with General de Gaulle shares the distinction of being one of the "two most impressive people" the young girl had met during those years. It is interesting to note that Berenson was gentle, philosophic, with a deep knowledge and appreciation of Renaissance art, while the French general had then, and still retains, the autocratic self-confidence, the rude intolerance and obsessive will of an imperialist.

How does a girl go about job hunting? Particularly if her parents are affluent and social, and the employer is well aware of the fact that the applicant will not starve if he turns her down? Her background may serve as a detriment. It would be difficult for the average employer to take seriously the request of a girl whose background was as glittering and glamorous as Jacqueline Bouvier's.

Nevertheless, Jacqueline longed ardently for a newspaper reporter's job, and her amiable, obliging Uncle Hugh used his influence to get her a hearing.

He telephoned his friend Arthur Krock. That distinguished member of *The New York Times* staff asked *his* friend, Frank Waldrop of the Washington *Times-Herald,* to grant the girl an interview.

Perhaps it is pertinent here to suggest that long before they met, the lives of Jacqueline Bouvier and John F. Kennedy were gradually converging toward a point of contact. For Arthur Krock counted also among his friends old Joe Kennedy and his son, the brilliant young John Fitzgerald. As for Waldrop, at a previous time Kathleen Kennedy had served as his secretary.

Mr. Waldrop was intrigued by the beauty of the wide-eyed applicant. He was impressed by her alert mind which was such an enchanting contradiction to the small-girl voice that in later years was to be compared to the late Marilyn Monroe's.

Nevertheless, he assumed a stern air. He wanted to know how serious was her interest in a career. Was it perhaps, he suggested drily, merely to span the time before she met a suitable young man?

Wide-eyed and earnest, Jackie assured him she was most serious about a professional future.

"If you're serious, I'll be serious," Frank Waldrop replied. She was told to come back after the holidays. However, he added, she was not to plan on working for six months and then blithely upset the applecart by getting engaged.

"No sir," Jacqueline said emphatically.

Shortly after the holidays, however, a sheepish young girl did find herself engaged.

Her little dressmaker, Mimi Rhea, reports that soon after the Christmas 1951 holidays, Jacqueline brought a fresh batch of new clothes to be fitted to her figure. During this period, she was buying frocks right off the rack and experimenting with styles that would be right for her tall-shouldered figure. That was the day she first wore an engagement ring.

The man Jacqueline had consented to marry was John G. W. Husted, Jr.

In announcing the engagement, the Washington *Times-Herald* reported:

"Her fiancé attended Summerfields School, Hastings, England and was graduated from St. Paul's School, Concord, New Hampshire, and Yale University. During the war he served with the American Field Service attached to the British forces in Italy, France, Germany and India. The wedding will take place in June."

Husted was an enormously attractive man, the son of a New York banker and was himself destined for the stock market. He was certainly a suitable mate for a girl of Jacqueline's background. The Husted relatives were delighted with the match.

Jacqueline spent several months commuting from Washington to New York. But her friends, among them the dressmaker who saw so much of her, had the uneasy feeling that the young woman was being guided by her cool, logical mind rather than her heart. The fact that it was a courtship whose proximity depended on each partner's willingness to spend the weekend in travel from New York to Washington, or the other way around, may have served as a damper to the romance. That in itself is apt to suggest that Jacqueline had not entirely committed her heart. For in due time, Jacqueline's family announced with protocol and reticence that "the engagement was ended by mutual consent."

The severance of an engagement brings to any girl a certain amount of shock, humiliation and soul-searching. From her Grandfather Bouvier, fortunately, Jacqueline had learned the balm of work. She went back to face Frank Waldrop who had cynically warned her that the engagement wouldn't last.

There was no opening on the paper for a reporter. He assigned her, therefore, to the job of "Inquiring Camera Girl." That he withheld her by-line did not cause her any concern or loss of face. Knowing the importance of proving oneself, she was confident it would eventually be granted to her.

She dressed simply for her job, in shirtwaist frocks, made with easy skirts. She was partial to plaids and checks, although her working uniforms included frocks of solid colors. One of her favorite outfits was a plaid slim-line skirt topped with a turtle-neck black sweater of the kind that is popular in France. Her accessories included low-heeled black pumps and an over-the-shoulder bag crammed with necessities of her trade—pencils, pads, flashbulbs.

During that period, she was sensibly aware of the value of a dollar, and although she never quibbled over price, she made it a point always to ask in advance the cost of a garment. The days of French creations from Givenchy and Dior and Chez Ninon were still in the future. Perhaps if some seer had told Jacqueline at that time that within a few years a thousand-dollar price tag for a state ball gown wouldn't shock her sensibilities, she would not have believed him.

Jacqueline's job on the paper consisted of a column of questions and answers accompanied by a snapshot of the person interviewed. The question was always topical—a necessity, the editor felt, for its purpose was to portray the beliefs of a cross section of the population. The questions ranged from serious to absurd. Although the editor considered the Inquiring Photographer an important column, most newspapermen, including staff photographers, shied away from it.

Jacqueline was no doubt on a trial basis. But if it gave her cause for worry, she serenely hid her feelings. Having assured Waldrop that she was expert with a camera, she looked up a school of photography and took an accelerated course. Thus, she worked while learning. As a matter of fact, a simple Brownie was a mechanism she understood, but the old Graphlex was a headache even for hardened professionals. However, she soon caught on to the techniques. The will to learn and the will to work were as much a part of her nature as the artistic talents.

The entire male staff of the *Times-Herald* was unusually cavalier with her. But with wry humor, she couldn't decide whether it was gallantry or gratification that the unwanted chore of the candid camera was off their own necks.

Jacqueline started off at a weekly salary of $42.50, which with subsequent small raises finally increased to $56.75. She was not an especially good photographer, but her imagination and humor made the column engaging. She preferred interviewing children for their candor and fresh viewpoint. But her best columns were devoted to public figures.

In view of subsequent events in Jacqueline Bouvier's life, it is ironic that her first subject should be Mrs. Richard M. Nixon.

Jacqueline's question was this: "Who will be Washington's Number One Hostess now that the Republicans are back in power?"

Mrs. Nixon, the perfectionist who during her husband's campaign for Presidency was sometimes described as the woman most symbolic of "The American Dream," replied carefully.

"Why, Mrs. Eisenhower, of course. I think her friendly manner and sparkling personality captivate all who see or meet her. She is equally gracious in small groups or long receiving lines, where she has the knack of getting acquainted with each person instead of merely shaking hands with the usual phrase, 'How do you do?' The people of America will always be proud of their First Lady."

Picture the meeting of these two young women. Jacqueline on her first job, a novice in spite of her family's position. Pat Nixon, already internationally known and admired as the wife of the new Vice President. Photographs of Jacqueline showed her taking fences on her favorite mare. Campaign pictures used extensively showed Pat Nixon pressing her husband's pants. But in our American culture, the idea of the rags-to-riches saga was soon to become obsolete. Men in high office were to come from the richest and most influential families of the country and most of them, products of the Ivy League schools, advanced thinking and perhaps a sense of guilt at the manner in which their robber grandfathers had accumulated fortunes, began to dedicate themselves to public service.

John Fitzgerald Kennedy was one of this new breed. Although he was an omnivorous reader, his capacity for intellectual growth did not show itself until his college days, when he was graduated *cum laude* from Harvard.

His early schooling ranged from the Dexter School, a private school in Brookline, Massachusetts, to the Riverdale School in suburban New York, and finally to Canterbury, a preparatory school at New Milford, Connecticut. Canterbury was the only Roman Catholic institution Jack attended. His grades were average, except in Latin which he found a stumbling block. He had, however, an extraordinary memory and the capacity for rapid reading. Only when it came to his belongings was he notoriously absent-minded. The way he misplaced socks, gloves and other possessions was a great trial to his orderly mother.

Mrs. Joseph Kennedy was a simple, direct, astonishingly beautiful woman who passionately loved the Church. She made it a point to take the children to services every day. It was not her intention to make her young ones Sunday Christians. She wanted them to understand that Christian ethics and morality were a way of life.

"You have to tend to the roots as well as the stems, and slowly and carefully plant ideas and concepts of right and wrong, religion and social implications and applications," she said.

But motherhood was no trial to her. Both her beauty and her character bloomed under the challenge of being a parent to such varied and assorted personalities. The task of molding the childish characters was primarily hers. Her husband was too busy building the fabulous fortune that was eventually to make his children and grandchildren free of financial insecurity and vindicate his own abilities, foresight and shrewd dealings.

It required all of Rose Kennedy's tact, skill and diplomacy to keep her noisy energetic competitive brood in reasonable harmony. She remained the eye of the storm, and Jack Kennedy, who seemed extremely sensitive to her mood, said, "She was a little removed and still is, which I think is the only way to survive when you have nine children. I thought she was a very model mother for a big family."

It is significant that the girl he married has the same capacity for being a little removed; perhaps it is, in another way, a self-survival gambit.

That the family was so clannish was due to Mrs. Kennedy's maternal skills. Her husband had deliberately encouraged the competitive spirit among the children, but it was Rose Kennedy who directed these feelings into acceptable and healthy channels. She stressed the importance of outdoor sports, and the children were athletes at an early age. On holidays, she managed to create the kind of program that would keep them in the sun and water all day and leave them in healthy exhaustion and ready for bed early in the evening. The children were receptive to her suggestions. Her attitude, more than their father's, bred within them a fierce loyalty toward each other. Indeed, they were so deeply integrated as a clan that outsiders often speculated if they would ever marry. Of course, in Ireland, sons are notoriously late to wed; they cling to the maternal hearth long after they are ripe for their own homes. The Kennedys seemed to repeat the pattern.

Although the Kennedys were after a fashion rootless, because of Joe's widely scattered business affairs, the big rambling house in Hyannis Port is a genuine port of home to them. Here, Rose has lodged some of her treasures, which include a fabulous collection of dolls in native costumes collected from all over the world. Tables are cluttered with framed autographed portraits of the world's great, including one of the late Pope Pius XII, who as a cardinal had been a visitor at the Kennedys'.

Rose was a devout Catholic in the most fundamentalist way. When in the summer of 1944, her gay and charming daughter Kathleen, married an English marquess, Billy Hartington, it was no time for maternal rejoicing for Rose. The entire Kennedy family withdrew in chill noncommunication for the press or their daughter who had found love outside her faith. Rose expected her children to follow her teachings and maintain their devout Catholicism. The daughters all attended parochial schools. Her fondest wish was that Teddy, her youngest son, would find a vocation in priesthood, since in most devout Irish families one son is often dedicated to spending his life in the celibate role of the priest. She devoted all her considerable energies to Catholic charities, and she was to receive recognition for her good works. The Cross of the Pro Ecclesia et Pontiface was awarded to her, as well as the title of Papal Countess. Rose Kennedy is one of the two American women to receive this honor.

Her son Jack had described his mother as a "religious woman in the true sense."

Even her husband, hard-bitten, tough Joe Kennedy admitted of his wife and children, "My wife is a deeply religious woman, and she may have given more time and care to their spiritual training than some mothers do."

So John Fitzgerald Kennedy's religious orientation was quite different from that of the girl he was to marry.

Although Jacqueline Bouvier stemmed on her father's side from French Roman Catholics, it appears that religion played much less of a role in her youth. Sunday school and the rituals of the Church were no doubt adhered to, but perhaps without the deep sense of identity that the Irish Catholics have with their priests and the Church itself.

Rose Kennedy found her faith a rich and comforting rock during the ensuing years when tragedy twice tested her capacity for faith.

Joseph Kennedy, Jr., was killed on a test mission in which the plane he piloted exploded in midair.

Nor was this the end of Rose Kennedy's calvary. At last, the family was forced to face realistically facts about the condition of their sister Rosemary. The sweet-natured childish young woman was incurably retarded. At the suggestion of innumerable doctors, the parents finally agreed she might be happier in an institution, rather than suffer from the inadequacies of trying to keep up with a bright energetic set of brothers and sisters.

Finally, there was the tragedy of Jack's accident in the PT boat in the South Pacific. He never fully recovered from his wounds. It was to take two serious spinal operations and a close encounter with death before the damage was sufficiently repaired so that he could continue with his life.

It was Rose who was her son's greatest booster and assistant when Jack began his campaign to sweep Henry Cabot Lodge out of his seat in the Senate. As a politicking mother, she was endowed with a touch of genius.

Naturally, the Kennedy millions as well as the Kennedy charm helped the contest.

"Jack knows the sorrow, the tears and the heartbreaking grief of loneliness that comes to a family when a mother has lost her eldest son," she told women voters. "So I know Jack will never get us into war."

Jack beat Lodge, and by 70,000 votes. With the Kennedy clan back of him, working like busy beavers, he was suddenly a powerful political force in the state.

John F. Kennedy didn't create a brilliant impression during his early years as a Congressman or Senator. Yet in spite of his gay bachelor life, his restlessness and his perfunctory duties to his office, there was the stirring of something deeper within his mind that was to come to fruition a decade later.

There is a foreshadowing of this depth of thought in his article for the Conde Nast magazine that was reprinted in 1963 in the anthology, "The World in Vogue."

The title: "Brothers, I Presume."

John Kennedy speaks of the basic antagonism between authors and politicians and seeks to defend the politicians.

"The American politician and the American literary man operate within a common framework—the framework of liberty," he wrote.

He continued by "calling again for recognition of how inextricably entwined are the professions and the fates of our politicians and writers. In this way, the synthesis of our efforts and talents may provide a greater service to the cause of freedom—a bulwark to meet the challenge of the future."

In these lucid remarks, we see the breadth and insight of the young Senator who wrote the Pulitzer Prize winning *Profiles In Courage*.

We see also the promise of the statesman he was to become in the last tragic year of his life.

The child who, later in life, was to be likened to John Wilkes Booth had a reasonable, normal babyhood. His mother, Mrs. Marguerite Oswald, managed to stay home and care for him for the first two years of his life. But it was a household crouched under the shadow of poverty and the lack of a male image. After his mother's marriage in May, 1945, to Edwin A. Eckdahl, an industrial engineer, Lee was taken out of the boardinghouse that had been a quondam home to him from the third year of his babyhood and brought to live with the newlyweds. The boy entered public school at seven, an older age than most children, and while he was subdued in class, he was active in sports and the boys in his class seemed to like him.

When Lee was eight, his stepfather sued his mother for divorce. Mr. Eckdahl claimed that she once tossed a bottle at his head and had struck him. He received the divorce.

During the following years, adults and children who had any contact with Lee felt he was antisocial, and often even vicious toward children his own age or younger.

Whenever he got into trouble that was reported to his mother, she loyally took his part. She never believed him capable of wrong doing. Since she spent her days at work, she tried, perhaps, to compensate for this necessary neglect by lavishing extra attention on him. But already he showed signs of ill-concealed anger and erratic behavior that were later to cause psychiatrists some grave concern about him.

Whenever he reached out for affection, he was usually rebuffed. Or perhaps, needing and fearing love, he rebuffed the kindness from various teachers and even willfully exploited it. A photograph of Lee Oswald at the age of twelve shows a thin youngster with the first indication of a tight, angry mouth that in later years was to become set in a sneer. He was already known as a roughneck, yet only a couple of years previously he had been capable of lavishing love and devotion on the family dog.

How does a man become a hater?

Dr. Bruno Bettelheim, the psychiatrist who is a professor at the University of Chicago, suggests that the germs of hate are within all human beings. But most of us learn to control these feelings during childhood. Most boys are helped to become decent human beings by the authority figure, which is usually the child's own father.

"Lee Oswald felt a deep need for external authority," Dr. Bettelheim wrote in an article in *Life* Magazine. "The most delinquent lad realizes at some level that his acts are as destructive to himself as they are destructive to others. Oswald enlisted in the Marines out of such a need for authority . . . but even this could not contain him. . . ."

Love is the most effective weapon against hatred, and this was a boy incapable of accepting himself; therefore, it was impossible for him to love any one else.

Lee Oswald, in his quest for self-acceptance, drifted to Russia and back, longed for the dictatorship of the father image of a Castro, shuttled pointlessly through his young erratic life to the final awful moment on the sixth floor of the old-fashioned building in Dallas.

He who had never had the living presence of his father developed an anger that grew in violence until it exploded in the destruction of a man—the man whose own father had worked with unflagging ambition and will to make his son the President of the United States.

Jacqueline Bouvier, like another photographer, Tony Armstrong-Jones, now Lord Snowden, successfully used a camera as the pathway to fame. Just as Tony was assigned to photograph Princess Margaret, the girl he later married, so was the Inquiring Camera Girl sent to photograph a promising young Senator from Massachusetts—John Fitzgerald Kennedy.

Her editor's orders were succinct. "Go up to the Hill and see this fellow. Tell him I sent you." Then with a wry smile he added, "You behave yourself. Don't get your hopes up. He's too old for you—besides, he doesn't want to get married."

Actually, Waldrop was quite aware of the rumors that Jacqueline had been seeing Senator Kennedy.

John and Jacqueline had first met at the home of Charles Bartlett, Washington correspondent for the Chattanooga *Times*. Bartlett was aware of the change in Jacqueline since her graduation from college. He was impressed by her new maturity and the sense of relaxation that seemed to bring her in closer contact to others.

"She was no longer the round little girl who lived next door," he said. "She was more exotic. She had become gayer and livelier." For months, Charles Bartlett and his wife, Martha, tried to bring the two young charmers to their home for dinner. Finally on the night of May 8, 1952, their efforts were successful.

Actually, four years previously, Jacqueline and John had met at a fashionable Long Island wedding. They were introduced, exchanged a few pleasantries, and then each went their way. The magnetic spark that was to bring them together years later had not yet been fanned.

However, the warm hospitality of the Bartletts, the young camera reporter's interest in her work, and the activities of the Hill and the young Congressman's feeling of relaxation worked the miracle of that evening.

Although John Fitzgerald Kennedy was not a snappy dresser—as a matter of fact, he seemed totally indifferent to the condition of his clothes—his boyish charm had a catnip effect on the girls of Washington.

Nor had the young Congressman entirely escaped the warm, loving care of his family. The elderly Kennedys, particularly his mother, felt perhaps that while John's mind was intent on his political future, he was careless of his health and physical person.

The parental, almost smothering concern, had shown itself while he was still at Choate. During his first year at the preparatory school, the elder Kennedys kept in close communication with George St. John, the headmaster. They were intensely interested in their second son's health and progress. Rose Kennedy wrote the school nurse, Miss Potts, asking her to make sure Jack took his medicine. Joseph Kennedy was perhaps more interested in the mark his son was to make upon the school. For, deep in his soul, he was infuriated by the Proper Bostonians' scorn for the lace-curtain Irish. A friend of the family suggests that few boys were as mothered and fathered as young John.

Nevertheless, in the full-page report that the headmaster of each cottage was required to write about new boys, there is this revealing comment about young Kennedy: "He is *all* boy."

Although Choate is headed by an Anglican clergyman, it is basically nondenominational. Jack attended Catholic services usually about once a week. In one letter to his mother, he wrote, "I received Communion this morning and am going to Church on Tuesday. I received the prayerbook and would you please send me a puff because it is very cold."

At Choate, he was an average student but was either bored with, or lacked aptitude in, languages. Latin and French frustrated him, and only in his final year at Choate did he evidently take a serious look at himself. He was deeply disappointed with the results. He confessed to his father that his talk about hard work was more fantasy than reality.

Old Joe Kennedy was not one to accept alibis, even when they were offered in a vein of humility. At that time the senior Kennedy was chairman of the Securities and Exchange Commission, and words of advice, though rendered in blunt, earthy language, came naturally to him.

". . . Now aren't you foolish not to get all there is out of what God has given you? After all, I would be lacking even as a friend if I did not urge you to take advantage of the qualities you have. It is very difficult to make up for fundamentals that you have neglected when you were very young and that is why I am always urging you to do the best you can. I am not expecting too much and I will not be disappointed if you don't turn out to be a real genius, but I think you can be a really worthwhile citizen with good judgment and good understanding."

Nevertheless, the father could not resist the temptation of affectionate bribes for good school reports. Today, of course, counselors in child psychology warn parents against such rewards, stressing the fact that the young should be indoctrinated with a love of study for its own intellectual benefits. But when Jack applied himself and his father was pleased, the result was apt to be a trip to England or a sailboat or a gift of comparable value.

While Jack was still at Choate, his father bought the Palm Beach estate, and Jack discovered girls—in Connecticut, Massachusetts and Florida. He was an exceedingly personable young fellow, with lean good looks, an outgoing manner, a contagious smile and an insouciance that girls found irresistible.

When Jack was graduated in 1935 from Choate, he was chosen as "The Boy Most Likely to Succeed."

Yet neither scholastically nor in sports were there any indications to substantiate their choice. In studies, Jack was sixty-fourth in a class of 112, and he never made varsity in sports. Perhaps the radiance—what his wife was later to call the shining light—was already evident. Certainly his charm, his disarming and witty self-deprecation were already in evidence.

As a young Congressman in Washington, he made little impression at first. Indeed, his manner of dress was so careless that he was sometimes mistaken for a page off duty or a tourist. Nevertheless, the young intellect was already absorbing knowledge; the mind, basically quick and alert, was readying itself for the future. By osmosis, he had absorbed much of what his extraordinary father had to transfer to his sons.

Joe Kennedy was a tough disciplinarian, a wily infighter. There was nothing of the brooding Irish poet in his nature. He believed in reality. He schooled his children in how to deal with the exigencies of the future.

As Ambassador to the Court of St. James, Joe Kennedy had a special press secretary, which was unusual in diplomatic circles. He was shrewdly aware of the importance of a cooperative and obliging press. It was an art that his family was to cultivate and which came into full bloom during the Presidency of his son.

In Washington, John leased a house in Georgetown and shared it with his sister, Eunice, who was then not yet married to R. Sargent Shriver, Jr. Eunice was then employed as executive secretary to the National Conference on Juvenile Delinquency. Their mother saw to it that they were well cared for by Margaret Ambrose, who had been part of the Kennedy staff for three decades. Thus, with all the comforts of home, with a career as a young and coming politician, with plenty of dates and a variety of girl friends, Jack had a pleasant, active life. But as in later years, he was already preparing for future goals—in this case, the election ahead. With the unflagging help of his family, particularly his mother, Rose, he graduated from Congress to the Senate. For the time, he seemed content. His stature grew less, however, from his records in the Senate than the immediacy of his own maturing nature.

It was at this moment in his life that he met the Inquiring Camera Girl at the dinner party specifically given for the two by Charles and Martha Bartlett.

Young Kennedy was in no hurry to get married; the comforts of home were his, but as he admitted later, after the first meeting at the Bartletts' he came to the conclusion that when he did decide to marry, this would be the girl for him.

However, that evening, which began auspiciously and continued with gaiety over dinner, ended in disaster.

Jacqueline was much taken with John Kennedy; his sense of humor reminded her of her father's. When Charles and John escorted Jacqueline to her car, it was the Senator's intention to go along with her and stop somewhere for a drink and more talk. Unfortunately, he noticed a man sitting in the back seat of her car. It escaped him that Jacqueline was equally startled and put out. The Bartletts' fox terrier, Josie, was the first to notice the intruder. In the confusion and embarrassment that followed Josie's pounce upon the friendly but uninvited guest, Jack Kennedy quietly took off.

Jacqueline never got a chance to explain to him that this little tableau was not of her planning.

Nor did she see him again for seven months.

It was a casual haphazard courtship. Like his father, John Kennedy was obsessed by a drive for worldly objectives. These were obstacles to the duties he would naturally have to assume as husband and father. Women were perhaps responsible for his casual attitude toward them; it is not in the male nature to treasure whatever comes easily.

Jacqueline's decision to break her engagement to young Husted stemmed from the fact that much of the courtship was conducted in absentia. But that plane and train romance was nothing compared to the casual way John F. Kennedy drifted in and out of her life.

An interim of seven months can amount to a lifetime. In such a time span, men can fall in love, marry impulsively, change careers, go off to war. Instead, the young Congressman was girding himself for his political battle with Henry Cabot Lodge.

Jacqueline and her sister, Lee, quietly took off for a summer abroad.

However, during the last weeks that John F. Kennedy was energetically campaigning for the Senate, politician and girl reporter did come together. Jacqueline, feminine and adroit, interviewed the Congressman, and possibly then explained that the man parked in the back seat of her car the night of the Bartlett dinner was merely a friend—an ex-friend. Or perhaps she kept quiet like the famous Elsie de Wolfe, who believed a woman should never explain anything!

Their first formal date took them to the Blue Room of the Shoreham Hotel. But Jacqueline's pleasure in the evening of good food and prospective dancing was somewhat dampened by the presence of a third party—a Massachusetts political figure.

After that, the pair saw each other often but discreetly, so as not to call public attention to their meetings. While John was canvassing innumerable dreary little Massachusetts factory towns for votes, he would call Jacqueline from a telephone booth and ask her for a date between his campaign stops. He would fly back to Washington for the weekend, and they would have dinner, go to the movies with their friends the Bartletts. Or with Jack's brother and sister-in-law, Bobby and Ethel Kennedy, they would play games—bridge or Monopoly.

But the pattern of their meetings was often broken by Jack's political obligations. Jacqueline would nearly give up at times any hope of hearing from him again. But then, while she was working in the city room of the newspaper in the middle of the week, a telephone call would come for her from Hyannis Port. Everyone would pause to listen discreetly, for the erratic romance was followed with enormous interest by a body of sideline fans. When Jacqueline in her childlike whisper would repeat, "Saturday?" the staff would breathe again in relief. All was going well for their handsome camera girl, who was something of a mascot to them. Most of the newspapermen had originally sought to date her, but she handled the invitations with such poise that they accepted her refusals without feeling hurt.

On one occasion, Kennedy's car broke down after he had seen Jacqueline home to "Merrywood." She offered him the use of her stepfather's car, and the next morning, Hugh Auchincloss found in the place of his own fine automobile a rather dilapidated car with a Massachusetts license.

When her editor sent her up the hill to interview the Senator, Jacqueline solemnly reported that John F. Kennedy had suggested she get other interviews before she recorded his.

So she asked a series of Senators and the Vice President what it was like to observe the Senate pages at close range. Then she switched the question and asked the pages, "What is it like to observe the public officials at close range?"

There was a humorous reason for her questions. Because of his youthful appearance, Senator Kennedy was sometimes mistaken for a page—and a carelessly dressed one.

To her question, the Vice President replied with his customary earnestness, "I would predict that some future statesman will come from the ranks of the page corps. During my time as a Senator, I noticed that they are very quick boys, most of whom have a definite interest in politics. I feel they could not get a better political grounding than by witnessing the Senate in session day after day as they do."

Senator Kennedy replied in a jocular vein:

"I've often thought that the country might be better off if we Senators and the pages traded jobs. If such legislation is ever enacted, I'll be glad to hand over the reins to Jerry Hoobler. In the meantime, I think he might be just the fellow to help me straighten out my relationship with the cops; I've often mistaken Jerry for a Senator because he looks so old."

Said Jerry Hoobler of Ohio:

"Senator Kennedy always brings his lunch in a brown paper bag. I guess he eats it in his office. I see him with it every morning when I'm on the elevator. He's always being mistaken for a tourist by the cops because he looks so young."

Jacqueline's column didn't always find acceptance with those interviewed or with their families.

One lady complained to the *Times-Herald* when her children were the victims of Jacqueline's camera and pen. She was Mrs. George G. Moore, sister of Mrs. Dwight D. Eisenhower. The two girls had been interviewed by the Inquiring Camera Girl as they were leaving for the day the John Eaton School in Washington. They answered frankly with childhood's typical lack of inhibitions. Jacqueline asked how their lives had been affected by their uncle's election to the Presidency.

Said eleven-year-old Ellen Moore, who sometimes earned extra pocket money as a baby-sitter: "I've been charging fifty cents an hour. Now that my uncle is President of the United States, don't you think I should get seventy-five?"

Ellen also spoke her mind on that bane of schooldays—homework. "A girl in my class said that when my uncle's President, I should tell the teacher to give me good marks or he'd throw her off the school board. But you know, I don't think that would do any good, because if Uncle Ike heard that, he'd tell my mother and would she get mad!"

Ten-year-old Mamie Moore complained: "Only three people in my class knew Uncle Ike was my uncle. None of the others would believe me. But I've got brown hair and bangs and everybody says I look like Auntie Mamie, so now they all know."

Thus, Jacqueline Bouvier, as a professional journalist, intruded on the private lives of VIP's, a form of conduct that she was to decry not too many years afterward when she was in the White House and zealously hoping to shield her children from the prying press.

During this period, she was seeing Jack Kennedy sporadically. Yet they had an understanding of sorts—they were engaged to be engaged. Jack was still altar-shy; it would take tact and femininity to guide him over the hurdle into the sunny field of matrimony.

Perhaps it became the eternal and unconscious tug of war between a bachelor and his girl. But Jacqueline, for all her shyness and little-girl whisper of a voice, was truly feminine, and the year in Paris under the warm wryly knowledgeable guidance of the Comtesse was a refresher course in femininity. A famous New York psychiatrist, Dr. Smiley Blanton, suggested recently that any girl can get the man she wants.

The young Senator often ate his paper-bag lunch in his office. Sometimes he forgot to bring it from home and skipped the midday meal altogether.

It was the most natural thing in the world for the Camera Girl to be in the Senate Chambers during the lunch hour, and nearly always she had her lunch with her. It was a hot box lunch, always ample for two people, and oddly enough often containing his favorite foods. A pleasant event of this nature can become a habit very quickly. If a girl were to miss showing up at the lunch hour for a day or two, a young man might get to miss her gay presence and her delicious picnic lunch.

Jacqueline did a thoroughly charming and enchanting brain-washing job, too, through the medium of her column.

Some of the questions she presented to passers-by included a pointed one: "Is your marriage a fifty-fifty partnership, or do you feel you give more?"

Another leading question: "Can you give any reason why a contented bachelor should get married?"

Or one even more challenging: "The Irish author Séan O'Faoláin claims that the Irish are deficient in the art of love. Do you agree with the author's opinion?"

None of these seemed to make a dent in Jack's bachelor armor, although he did invite her to the Eisenhower Inaugural Ball in January, 1953. Jack was utterly cavalier in his manner to her, inviting her to meet his regiment of relatives, sending her the most thoughtful gifts, taking her everywhere. But did he ask, "Will you marry me?" Not that hardened young bachelor! After six months of courtship, Jacqueline perhaps decided that absence might make him aware of her as a possible wife.

Outsiders, unaware of her decision, knew only that she seemed to be losing her zest for journalism because of her romance with Senator Kennedy. So her friends were considerably surprised when she took off the last minute for the coronation of Queen Elizabeth II. It was ostensibly an assignment for her paper; her private feelings have never been disclosed, although she did confide to a newspaper friend during that period, "What I want more than anything else in the world is to be married to him."

Indeed, a friend was partly responsible for the impulsive trip. Aileen Bowdoin, with whose two younger sisters Jacqueline had made her first trip to Europe, telephoned to ask if Jacqueline would like to go with her. They had two days only before boarding the *Queen Mary*.

Jacqueline agreed to send back stories for her newspaper; family friends gave the girls the use of an apartment in London.

They were invited to the U.S. Embassy, to hostess Perle Mesta's jumbo dance, and were provided escorts and even seats at a vantage point for the coronation procession.

Jacqueline filed dispatches that were models of wit and charm. She achieved a journalistic success. Of "Mesta Fiesta," as she dubbed the gala event in Londonderry House, she informed her readers that "Lauren Bacall was the belle of the ball . . . She had a swooping waltz with General (Omar) Bradley, then a series of romantic foxtrots with the Marquess of Milford Haven (Prince Philip's best man). She wore a tight white lace dress and her long scarlet fingernails rested lightly on his highly burnished epaulets. Bogie, wearing a plain old white-tie-and-tails outfit, cut in on her."

Jacqueline's amusing cartoon to illustrate the story depicted Lauren's husband, the late Humphrey Bogart, descending upon the handsome Marquess. She managed to extract from a friend of Prince Philip the tidbit that it had been necessary to place a special mark upon the crown of St. Edward the Confessor, which would be used during the ceremony, to ensure its being placed in the right position upon the Queen's head. At the coronation of her father, George VI, it had been put on backwards.

Ladies-in-waiting confided to the enthusiastic young reporter that on Coronation Day it was necessary for them to have their hair dressed at three in the morning, for they were due at Westminster Abbey at 6:30 A.M.

Like all of Washington, young Senator Kennedy read her witty reports. Her work impressed him. But the suggestion of the gay social life that held her in London evidently irritated him. A girl like Jacqueline is not unattended; her lively accounts of the theater and dancing at the fashionable night clubs suggested a host of admirers.

He wired her: "Articles excellent but you are missed."

From the cautious young Senator, this was practically a declaration of love.

Jacqueline missed him no less. She spent her spare time combing bookstores, searching for volumes to please him. When she brought them home, there was a hundred dollars in overweight charges to be paid. But Jack was there to greet her, and that was the day he finally asked her to marry him.

Shortly afterward, Jacqueline Bouvier resigned her job as the Inquiring Camera Girl. But she made new headlines on June 25, 1953, when her engagement to Senator John Kennedy was officially announced.

Her father's sister, her adored Aunt Maudie, had known of the good news for some time. But she had been sworn to secrecy out of consideration for the *Saturday Evening Post* editors who had scheduled an article: "Jack Kennedy—The Senate's Gay Young Bachelor."

A few years later, her White House secretary, Tish Baldrige, was to quip that Jacqueline Kennedy was the girl who had everything, including Jack Kennedy.

This was the girl who had once feared nobody would want to marry her.

Chapter Four

The ninth month of the year is not the favorite bridal month, but the wedding that took place September 12, 1953, rivaled for pomp and beauty the bridals that took place in June.

The wedding of Jacqueline Bouvier and Senator John F. Kennedy was celebrated with a nuptial mass at St. Mary's Church on Spring Street in Newport, Rhode Island. The ceremony indicates that Jacqueline, like her husband, was a practicing Catholic.

The day was bright and sunny. There was a stiff breeze at times that was playful with the flowers on the small tables set out for the bridal luncheon at Hammersmith Farm, the scene of so many childhood memories for the bride.

Jacqueline's wedding gown was of faille, the color of pale rich cream, with a snug bodice and a bouffant skirt. The bridal veil was of fragile rose-point lace and had been worn by Jacqueline's maternal grandmother, Mrs. James T. Lee, at her wedding. Part of the veil was shaped like a beanie, held in place on the crown of Jacqueline's head with sprigs of orange blossoms. The bridegroom had given her a magnificent diamond bracelet besides her engagement ring, which was composed of two stones—an emerald and a diamond. Her mother had lent her a lace handkerchief, and she had borrowed a blue garter, so the ecstatic bride—once a nonconformist—had blissfully followed the usual bridal ritual: something borrowed, something blue. Her bridal bouquet was a mixture of tiny spray orchids, miniature gardenias and stephanotis.

The attendants' gowns were of pale pink taffeta, set off by claret sashes. Lee Bouvier wore a slightly darker sash. Half sister Janet Jennings Auchincloss was the youngest of the bridesmaids, and her brother, Jamie, made an attractive page in a white silk shirt with a jabot and brief black velvet shorts. There were some indulgent observers who felt that Jamie stole the show.

As a point of interest, it might be mentioned that Jacqueline's dress, like her bridesmaids', had been made by her mother's Negro dressmaker. (Mary Todd Lincoln's favorite dress and mantua maker was a Negro woman by the name of Elizabeth Keckley.)

Photographs taken by Toni Frissell, the society photographer whose work appears in all the high-fashion magazines, shows a young man in formal attire, a flower in his buttonhole; a young man with a shock of heavy hair, a rather thin face, bland and innocent as an altar boy's, particularly around the jaw; looking in general on the sunny side of youth, far less than his actual thirty-seven years. His bride is almost his height, and her features are delicate, her expression radiant. It is characteristic of the pictures to appear of the couple in future years that while he is facing the camera, she is looking at him.

The exception is that last color photograph which the nation is long to remember, ten years, two months and a few days later, and shown full page in *Life* Magazine. Here Jacqueline is looking more toward the camera, while the President, oddly enough, is looking away from it. Perhaps the brilliant sunshine and the tumultuous greetings of the crowd have dazzled them out of their usual reactions to photographers. Jacqueline is holding a bouquet of roses, large, perfectly formed bright red roses, cradled like a child in her left arm, and in contrast to the strawberry pink of her Chanel-type suit.

If one contrasts this photograph with the set of bridal pictures, one finds the record of a decade of growth written on their faces. Not only growth in the trials and adjustments of marriage, but in the shaping of their natures, in the tempering of character that contributed to their world wide image as the symbol of a young, energetic, vigorous America.

The President has lost his lean and hungry look. The medications for the adrenal deficiency that plagued him for a while have added a kind of squirrel fullness to the once gaunt cheeks; his body is a man's, erect and powerful; the smile, even at its warmest, has a touch of the quizzical, a suggestion of sorrow as if this were a man who knew that life has its balances and all that is received must be paid for in full.

But Jacqueline looks astonishingly young; of course, she is barely thirty-four, and the fashions she has helped to create throughout the country, and of which she is the leading exponent, are youthful; their emphasis on the small-girl quality has enchanted the world. The brown hair with its touch of chestnut falls in a loose, near-shoulder-length wave with a lock over the forehead. The pillbox, of the same strawberry material as the suit, perched insouciantly on the crown of her head, adds to the impression of gay spirits. It might be a photograph of any member of the fabulously rich, gypsy jet set who makes a home of a plane, a cabana, a houseboat, a leased villa. The porcelain Dresden-china look that Cholly Knickerbocker found enchanting in the debutante has been transformed into a continental sophistication. Only the smile, wide and spontaneous, reveals the fact that the imaginative little girl is still alive.

The two who came together in marriage that day in Newport were to suffer all the beauty and tragedy of wedded life, its petty miseries and majestic unity.

But what held them together, perhaps, was the intuitive recognition that their need for each other would be durable and enduring.

Archbishop Richard J. Cushing, here from Boston to celebrate the nuptial mass, read a special apostolic blessing sent by His Holiness, Pope Pius XII.

> "The Holy Father, on the occasion of this marriage, cordially imparts to the Honorable John Fitzgerald Kennedy and Mrs. Kennedy his paternal apostolic blessings in pledging enduring Christian happiness in married life."

The ceremony lasted forty minutes, during which time Mrs. George Maloney played traditional wedding music on the organ. Jacqueline was given in marriage by her step-father, Hugh Auchincloss, and Robert Kennedy—later to become Attorney General of the United States—was the boyish-looking best man. The church was attractively decorated with white chrysanthemums and gladioli.

There were six hundred friends in St. Mary's for the ceremony and hundreds of others had been invited for the reception at Hammersmith Farm.

Hugh Auchincloss' estate was the most appropriate setting for a romantic wedding. Thousands of wedding presents were on display. Meyer Davis, who had played at the wedding of Jacqueline's parents, brought his fifteen-piece orchestra. The Senator and his newly acquired lady led the dancing to the tune of "I Married an Angel." Marion Davies, former screen star and friend of the Kennedys, was among the prominent guests.

The elaborate wedding cake was the gift of a baker who was a fervent Kennedy admirer. His first intention was to make the elaborate confection in the form of an "ocean of love" crowned with waves and with doves mounting the entire culinary masterpiece. Fortunately, Mrs. Hugh Auchincloss was able to persuade him to exchange his original plan for a more conventional one.

In an atmosphere of sheer bliss, Rose and Joseph Kennedy were noticeably happy. Mrs. Kennedy, looking much too young to be the mother of the Senator, wore a becoming blue lace gown. After the luncheon was over, the Kennedys joined the bride and groom and Mr. and Mrs. Auchincloss in the receiving line. It took two hours and twenty minutes for them to receive the congratulations and good wishes of all the guests.

By that time, all of the bridal party was justifiably weary.

The prenuptial celebrations began five days previously with a party given by the Kennedys for all the wedding guests. The Kennedys, who stressed vigor, gave their guests a fantastic workout of touch football, swimming, sailing, tennis, picnicking, scavenger hunts and charades—the last named being a game at which the hosts were justly famous. Joe's brood always played to win.

During the pre-wedding festivities, Jacqueline joined the family, even though the games were often much too rough and strenuous for her. As a matter of fact, John F. Kennedy appeared on his wedding day with a scratched face that created some humorous comments. The truth was that the scratches occurred when, during an enthusiastic game of touch football, he had fallen into a patch of roses.

Yet the rare times when Jack and Jackie could be together, without family patronage, their understanding began to mature. They walked along the beach in the long lovely sunlight; they sailed—just the two of them—and the horizons seemed to seal off the rest of the world. In those cherished moments they discovered a unity and tranquillity of spirit that were to give them a deep spiritual strength when the going got rough.

For the first time in her life, Jacqueline became more deeply aware of the daily obligations involved in the life of a devout Catholic. The Kennedys were practicing Catholics, deeply dedicated to their faith and with the rare ability to allow its spiritual values to determine the pattern of their behavior. This reaction was somewhat unfamiliar to Jacqueline, but once she was indoctrinated, her response was immediate and glowing.

She had discovered within herself the simple faith of a child, and evidence of that extraordinary faith is reflected on her radiant face as she and Jack exchanged vows. No matter how the future events shaped themselves, this was the man she was to love through life and death.

After the bride tossed her bouquet from the top of the stairs, she changed quickly into a gray going-away suit. The emerald green hat she had chosen as an accessory didn't please her, so she carried it.

The young couple flew to Acapulco, where they honeymooned in an enchanting pink cottage that overlooked the breakers of the blue-green Pacific.

Love in a tenement may have the same fierce intensity as love in a hundred-dollar-a-day suite. But there is no evidence to disprove that during the honeymoon at least, richer is better. A romantic setting, the heavenly blue of the sky meeting with the horizon, the blessings of the romantic Mexican waiters in the little out of the way restaurants, the dance to a Mexican band and the stroll through moon-drenched, sweetly scented paths to the cottage, with no outside intrusions, made the days for the young Kennedys a time of remembrance. Years later, after the trials of being the President's Lady had made some assaults on her sensitive nature, Jacqueline often felt that Shangri-La was not in the Orient nor even at Camp David.

Shangri-La was a cottage high above the blue-green sea in Acapulco.

When Lee Harvey Oswald realized that the answer to his troubled spirit was not to be found in the Marine Corps, he began his restless search again. This time it led him to Russia. It is often characteristic of emotionally unhappy men, who lack a healthy relationship with the father image or any man in authority who may substitute for that image, to keep seeking new resources for opportunity and self-appeasement.

Russia gave him no more satisfaction than the country he had renounced. Even his courtship had an unhealthy distorted origin. He met Marina Nikolaevna Pruskova, an attractive nineteen-year-old girl who worked in a hospital. The date was April 30, 1961. After seeing her for six weeks, he decided to marry her. Not out of love for Marina, but simply because the girl he really wanted had rejected him.

He was not a good husband, any more than he was a whole human being. Some of his anger at society found an outlet on the person of his vulnerable young wife. He denied her any form of independence. It is reported by friends that he once beat her for smoking, and that she left him for two days but decided to return.

He defected from Russia, and evidently the Communists were glad to see the last of him. He brought Marina and his first-born back to the United States, and there, through the good intentions of a Quaker, a young woman who believed in practicing the virtues of true Christianity, he found the temporary haven that was to direct him that ghastly day in November, 1963, to the sixth floor of the Dallas Book Repository.

The tapestry of fate is woven of so many near broken threads.

The greatest romances develop in time a certain monotony.

This is in its essence the strength and weakness of marriage. Only when two people have weathered a life together do they discover the variety and fresh joys in shared experiences that are denied the Don Juan or the Lorelei. In a happy union, even the periods of boredom that come on from familiarity are a kind of healthy restorative. One may find peaks of excitement with a stranger, but the joys of overt emotions take on a deeper delight when shared by a familiar partner, for unfamiliarity so often excites the senses that true feelings are not savored.

Surely Jacqueline Kennedy knew when she married Jack that she was marrying the frail sickly boy, the dashing young Congressman, the determined young Senator, and the succession of future images he was to be.

That it would not be an easy marriage she already knew even before the vows were exchanged. She had confided earlier to a friend her inner qualms that this marriage would take considerable working out.

There was, for instance, the differences in ages. Her husband was twelve years her senior. A wife, even with a mate her own age, has a tendency to be submissive, a quality that is perhaps intensified in a greater differential. And Jacqueline had been an independent little girl.

Then, too, her husband was not a relaxed individual. The race for Senate had been exhausting, and in spite of his warm smile and friendly manner, his hands were often tensely gripped. He suffered considerably from an old war injury to his back, and although he never complained, pain made him irritable.

In even the most tranquil mating of similar personalities, adjustments of marriage are exacting. In spite of her passionate, submissive love for her husband, it was a sore time for Jacqueline Kennedy. She was too much of an individualist to keep making adjustments that were foreign to her nature.

She did make a number of loving concessions out of her devotion to Jack and her growing desire to please her new in-laws. Take the matter of sports, for instance. Although she was a superb horsewoman, she learned how to become a member of the Kennedy team, which sports-wise meant a rugged style that also worked off physically any hidden angers and tensions. She played touch football—for a while only; she sailed and beachcombed; she learned to water ski; she acclimated herself to the noisy frenetic family circle, which never seemed to lose a single member of the clan and drew into their midst the newly minted marriage partners.

It was a marriage of contrasting personalities and backgrounds.

Jacqueline's was Old Guard, thoroughbred horses and silver trophies in the tack room, French antiques, art and literature, picnic hampers of vin rosé and eggs in aspic.

Jack's was politics, lace-curtain Irish, but with a will to overcome the immigrant background, politics, sudden unbelievable wealth through financial dueling, politics, peanut-butter sandwiches, politics.

As devotedly as Jacqueline loved her husband, acceptance of the political demands of his job was something of an ordeal for her. Worse still was the fact that he was comfortable in the political milieu and thrived on its disciplines. In the early days of their marriage, she was sometimes visibly bored with their political way of life. Once, while Jack was the center of a spontaneous admiring crowd, Jacqueline was seen in the back seat of their nearby car, restless and annoyed, as she waited for him. At no period of her marriage did she appear to find politics stimulating.

But early in the game, she was too inexperienced to hide her feelings.

Fortunately, she was much taken with her new regiment of in-laws.

As a family group, the Kennedys can be somewhat intimidating—it is almost as though the globe were bisected into two areas: that of the Kennedys and that of the rest of the world. Against such a formidable display of togetherness, there is often no weapon. But instinctively, the new daughter-in-law played it cool.

She was the only one who dared talk back to old Joe Kennedy, whose temper his brood deferred to. She was much taken with Jack's sisters, particularly Jean. Brother Bobby, perhaps, because he was so close to her husband, was the one to whom she was truly devoted.

"My son was rocked to political lullabies," Rose Kennedy once told a group of reporters.

If this maternal bunting had a sardonic effect on her daughter-in-law, it was never acknowledged by either party. Perhaps Jacqueline was in the early days doubly grateful for the political efforts of his mother and sister in working toward her husband's political future. All she wanted was a little more time with him. To have him share in the arts she loved; in the essence of her unique interests.

Once, somewhat impatient in her need for his company and deeply disturbed by his exhaustion, Jacqueline asked her husband why he had to work so hard. The expression on his face precluded the need of an answer.

It was a question she never again voiced.

At first the newlyweds, always on the move, were happy in rented houses or those of their immediate family. A Senator's life, Jacqueline soon found out, was not always spent in Washington.

She seldom talked politics with her husband; it was her belief that at home, he was entitled to distractions from his work. Although she was artistically gifted and not disposed to the less glamorous parts of housekeeping, she believed that home-making was not obsolete. Her primary desire was to create a warm, loving nest for her husband and children, although there were no indications as yet of a future family.

To be the wife of a Senator soon indicated a kind of life in a political goldfish bowl. Jacqueline however managed in the early years of marriage to remain in the background. Her husband was away a good deal, attending to the seeding of his political future. When he was at home, she considered it her task to help him relax—an art that even his close relatives had been unable to achieve.

Mrs. Burch Bayh, wife of the Senator from Indiana, has said, "I would not trade being a politician's wife for anything in the world."

This was not, perhaps, a reasonable facsimile of Jacqueline's feelings. No doubt, she could've got along very well without politics, except that it was the career her husband loved best, and it used up the considerable energies he had to expend in order to be happy. Later, he was to discover that an informed, cultivated and highly attractive wife was an enormous political asset and Jacqueline gallantly electioneered with him.

Although women were to read avidly about her clothes, her charm, her talents as a hostess, there is no doubt that by osmosis she was to make them more aware of politics as an important status career in contemporary American life.

The first winter following their marriage, Jacqueline found ample time to continue her art work and education. She enrolled at the Georgetown School of Foreign Service to study history. Although she preferred European background, especially French, she concentrated on American history, although she has since remarked that "American history is for men." Her husband was enormously touched by her gesture and Jacqueline was later to find it a most valuable experience.

She continued to study languages, too, although her French and Spanish were already fluent. This decision also proved to be foresight. For when the Kennedys dined at the United States Embassy in Rome in the summer of 1955, Clare Boothe Luce, our Ambassador, had invited among the guests George Bidault. Afterward, Kennedy and Bidault were eager to talk, but there was a language barrier.

Jacqueline was called on to act as an interpreter. Afterward M. Bidault wrote her a charming letter, which said in part, "I have never seen so much wisdom adorned with so much charm."

Nevertheless, those early years were an ordeal by marriage. In order to see her husband, Jacqueline was forced to accompany him on speaking tours. It was then that she learned the trick of packing quickly and having on hand clothes for every climate and occasion.

The togetherness of the Kennedy clan was both a joy and a trial to her. One of her close friends was her sister-in-law Jean, who has said, "Like most young brides, she looked forward to a more or less normal life. She probably wanted to have a home and to have her husband in it. I think it was difficult for her to make the adjustment to the kind of life she has had to lead, but she did make it, and without feeling sorry for herself."

This is perhaps an understatement that is in itself a tribute to Jacqueline's tact and adaptability. For their marriage served all too clearly to show up the difference in their backgrounds and tastes.

The sheer physical exuberance of the Kennedy clan was in itself somewhat wearing for a young woman who had a need of moments of introspection and spiritual solitude. But after a while, the Kennedys grew not only to accept the difference but to be proud of it.

During their first years together, Jacqueline and her husband both had a near encounter with death.

Shortly after their marriage, the Senator's health gave his wife and family grave anxiety. From his youth, Jack had a long history of back trouble. He had presumably ruptured a disk in the lower spine while playing football. This happened at Harvard where his older brother, Joe, had made the varsity football team. Jack had the will to equal his brother's prowess, but not the physical build. He made the junior varsity but at grave cost to his back.

Later, during World War II, the injury was aggravated when Jack was commanding a PT boat. A Japanese destroyer sliced the boat in half. Jack was thrown roughly to the deck. Afterward, he was in the chilly waters for five hours, during which time he towed a seriously injured crewman for three miles to shore. All the boyhood summers of swimming and sailing off Hyannis Port proved of help then, for Jack plowed through the water for excruciating miles, holding the wounded man's life jacket between his teeth. If this were not enough, he later swam back and forth rounding up the survivors of his crew and giving them something of his own humorous, biting wit to serve as a bulwark against physical and emotional collapse. But the experience was traumatic, and was to cost him seven years of future illness, during which time he never once gave up that indomitable Kennedy will to carry on.

But after his return from the Pacific to convalesce in the United States, John Kennedy was never completely free from excruciating spinal pain. He had always been lean but now he was a mere skeleton, weighing only 127 pounds. Doctors couldn't come to a unanimous decision on a procedure to correct his injury. A spinal fusion was suggested, but the medical men were afraid that Jack would not withstand the effects of this tricky, dangerous operation. He was then suffering from an adrenal deficiency which made the odds against his recovery unpredictable. At that time, the young Kennedy had bought an estate near the Auchincloss home in McLean, Virginia. The problem of commuting, while he was in pain and on crutches most of the time, made their first honeymoon home a nightmare for him.

Jack finally decided on the operation. He said, looking grimly at the crutches, "I'd rather die than spend the rest of my life on these things."

And die he nearly did.

It looked then as though Rose and Joseph Kennedy might have to endure the loss of another son. For in 1944, Jack submitted to surgery at a Massachusetts Naval Hospital, to ease the awful pressure on the sciatic nerve and to relieve muscular spasm. The results were not as good as had been anticipated.

On October 21, 1954, thirteen months after their marriage, Jack Kennedy entered the Hospital for Special Surgery in New York for a dangerous lumbar spine operation. There was a chance that he would not survive.

To have suffered such a risk and to meet with failure must have been a shattering blow not only to the patient but to his wife and his family. To add to the shock, Jack developed a fever. Infection had set in. One night he was so low that his family was summoned. Last rites were administered. But by morning, it looked as though he might barely survive.

Death had been a constant companion in the life of this lively, energetic and courageous young man.

After a six-week convalescence in Florida during which his strength got a booster shot, he returned North for a second operation. This one proved successful. A health bonus was a referral to Dr. Janet Travell, a woman doctor who greatly helped his muscle spasms with shots of Novocain.

During the long, discouraging days in the hospital and afterward during the Florida convalescence, Jacqueline was the sun in the gloom of his sickness and depression.

There were nurses and attendants, of course. But it was Jacqueline who made his days bearable. To keep a man so physically dynamic immobilized meant that she had to substitute other resources. "He was so brave always," she has said. His courage heightened her own determination to keep him interested and occupied. She was always there to bolster his spirit. She made herself useful as a loving therapist. She read to him and wrote notes for him. She made his calls. She was beside him, encouraging and gently humorous, as he took his first few steps. She haunted old bookstores for volumes of history that would appeal to him. She encouraged the visits of friends who might be entertaining.

The nights were especially difficult for him. He found the elderly competent nurses rather tedious. One evening, Jacqueline brought in a handsome blonde, who announced cheerily, "I'm the new night nurse."

It was Grace Kelly, now Princess Grace of Monaco.

The Senator's morale was understandably improved.

Perhaps it was his deep love of history, a carry-over from the boyish dreams of knights in armor; perhaps it was the interest compounded by the rare books his wife managed to track down for him. Perhaps it was triggered by his self-knowledge that a long convalescence was for so active a man a dangerous period. Whatever the reason, Jack began to make plans for a book on political courage.

There are in the footnotes of American history forgotten incidents of the most extraordinary displays of personal integrity. Jack had read of one such incident the previous year, and it had lingered in his mind. It was the story of Kansas Senator Edmund G. Ross, who was serving his first term after the Civil War. Ross kept faith with his own judgment by voting against the impeachment of President Andrew Johnson. He ignored political pressures and saved the President. But the act resulted in his political suicide.

Ambitious though he was, this was just the sort of gallantry that appealed to Jack Kennedy. With the help of Theodore Sorensen and Jacqueline, he collected material to weave the story of eight great Americans: John Quincy Adams, Daniel Webster, Thomas Hart Benton, Sam Houston, Edmund G.

Ross, Lucius Quintus Cincinnatus Lamar, George W. Norris, and Robert A. Taft.

The book was prefaced by a quotation from Edmund Burke's speech in praise of Charles James Fox for his attack on the East India Company in the House of Commons in 1783.

He well knows what snares are spread about his path, from personal animosity . . . and possibly from popular delusion. But he has put to hazard his ease, his security, his interest, his power, even his . . . popularity . . . He is traduced and abused for his supposed motives. He will remember that obloquy is a necessary ingredient in the composition of all true glory; he will remember . . . that calumny and abuse are essential parts of triumph . . . He may live long, he may do much. But here is the summit. He never can exceed what he does this day.

Profiles in Courage was published in 1956 by Harper and Brothers. It was to win for Jack the Pulitzer Prize for biography. The prize money went to the United Negro College Fund. Senator Kennedy was already aware of the importance of education for the country's second-class citizens.

Jack Kennedy was desperately ill for eight months. But it was a sickness that brought vitality and health and understanding to his marriage.

And the ordeal of his illness had encouraged all the latent tenderness and womanliness in his wife.

The dedication of his book was for her, but the emotional debt he owed her was one that would be compounded with love and respect over the years to come.

Nor was Jacqueline free from physical misfortunes.

Within four years, she was to have three Caesarian operations.

She suffered a miscarriage in 1955, and the following year her baby girl, a month premature, was dead. This child is now buried beside her father at Arlington Cemetery.

Jacqueline gravely overtaxed her strength during the stress of the 1956 Democratic National Convention when her husband narrowly missed out on the Vice Presidential nomination. As a result, she had nearly lost her life in giving birth to the baby.

Much loving anticipation had gone into the planning for the child's arrival. At last the Kennedys had bought a family kind of house, near Jacqueline's beloved Merrywood. The estate was named "Hickory Hill." The rooms were spacious; there was an airy nursery; there were stables for her horses, a swimming pool, and even an orchard.

When the baby was stillborn, everything about Hickory Hill seemed hollow and meaningless. Eventually Robert and Ethel Kennedy took possession of it, for it was ideal for their rapidly expanding family of children and pets. For a while, the lively Bob Kennedy brood kept a pet seal, Sandy, in the swimming pool, before they were finally persuaded to donate him to the Washington Zoo.

It could not have been easy for Jacqueline, with her love of children and need for them, to be the wife of a Kennedy, since to the other Kennedys large families seemed to come naturally and without complication. There is a strong emotional withdrawal for a woman after the loss of a child, particularly if it is followed by the incident of yet another stillborn infant. There must have been moments in the post-pregnancy melancholy when Jacqueline wondered if the fates would ever bless her with motherhood. Surely her prayers to the Virgin Mother included supplication for her own needs and for Jack's. He was equally anxious for children.

Yet withal, no bitterness or rebellion against God's wisdom marred her serene outlook. She even managed to retain her humor. One wedding anniversary, she created a series of whimsical sketches that totaled up the anguish both husband and wife had experienced in their trial years.

The sketches were titled, "How the Kennedys Spoil Wedding Anniversaries." They portrayed a series of hospital beds. In the first one, Jack was the occupant and his wife sat beside him. In the second, their roles were reversed. During the first seven years of their marriage, they were indeed often separated by politics or illness.

It was a marriage that did not blend into a smooth-flowing whole until after Jack became President of the United States.

Yet even before that, there was a gentling of Jacqueline's French nature. An early flowering of tact and compassion is revealed in a letter that came to light recently.

According to a report in a recent issue of the *National Observer*, Ronald C. Munro of Birmingham, England, once wrote her an ardent protest against the money the Kennedys were reported to have thrown away on a big party. "I added the facetious remark," Munro said, "that if they had so much money to scatter about, she could send me some and I would make better use of it."

Jacqueline personally replied to Mr. Munro.

"I received your letter and it has made me most unhappy these past few days. How wonderful it would be if this were a world where 7,000 pounds or $20,000 were merely to me the amount spent on an evening party, as you put it. If that were true, I would give what I could to enable you and your family to start a new life.

"The word 'millionaire' has a magic ring to it, but I think there are probably left in the world only a few maharajahs who could throw money around like that.

"I could not possibly give you that amount of money, were you my closest friend or relative. True, my husband is well off, but taxes in this country are enormous . . . and when he has paid for the household expenses and his business expenses, which are very great indeed, he does give to charity and that goes to the Kennedy Foundation for underprivileged children, . . . and at the end, there is not just a great pile of money lying around as you imagine. . . .

"From your letter, I think you have something that a great many rich people don't have, and would give their fortune to acquire, a wife and family who adore you and whom you love. . . ."

For several years, Munro kept the letter and eventually sold it to a New York firm of autograph dealers for $74. When it was auctioned in March, 1964, Alvin J. Slater, a Boston lawyer, bought it for $3,000—more money than a letter from any living woman has ever fetched at auction. Slater told the Boston *Globe's* Richard J. Connolly that he "did it because the letter appealed to his compassion. . . . It shows that this is a very rare, a great woman."

At the time she wrote it, Jacqueline Kennedy was twenty-six years old.

Another man has a treasured note from Jacqueline Kennedy. He is Millard A. Dorsey of Washington, D.C. Some time in the summer of 1954, Mr. Dorsey was buying a ticket at the Palace Theatre in Washington, when he saw a handsome young couple who were evidently short of the admission price. Mr. Dorsey recognized the young Senator from Massachusetts and spoke to him. John F. Kennedy had only a dollar and eighty-five cents with him. He was short of the fifteen

Mr. and Mrs. John V. Bouvier and daughter Jacqueline; picture was taken August 12, 1934.

United Press International Photo

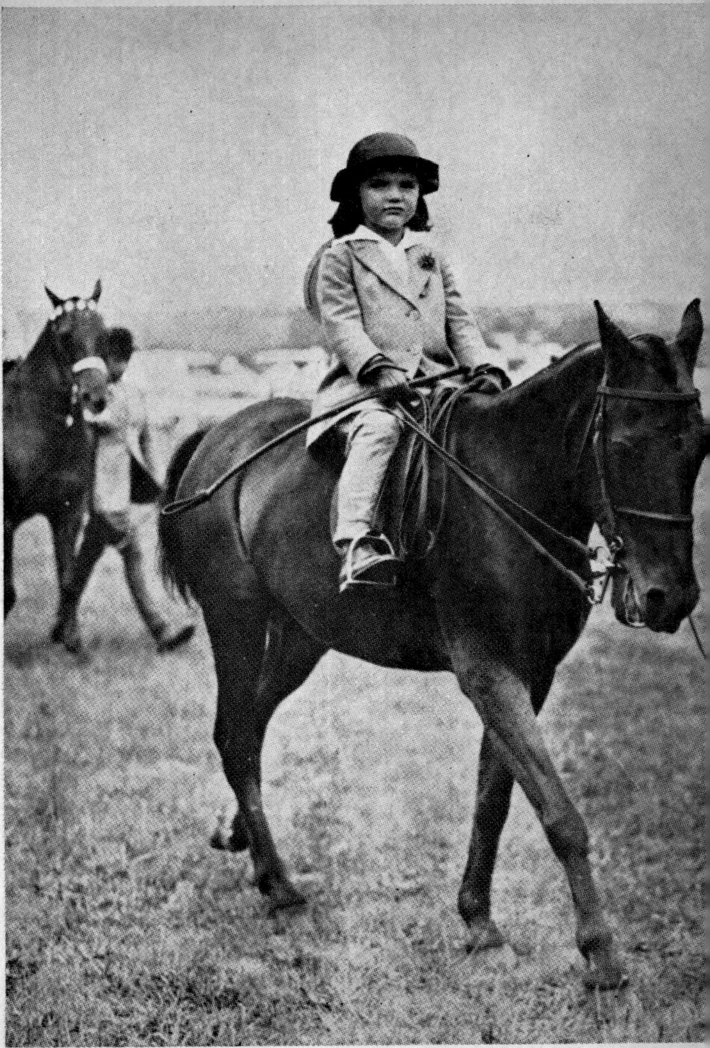

United Press International Photo

Jacqueline Kennedy competing in the Sixth Annual Horse Show of the Southampton Riding and Hunt Club, August 11, 1934.

United Press International Photo

United Press International Photo

Above: Aboard the *De Grasse* at sailing time, Jacqueline (center) is with a group of college girls who plan to live and study in France for a year.

Left: Jacqueline Kennedy as an inquiring photographer for the *Washington Times-Herald.*

Wide World Photos

Taking a short stroll by the Kennedy home at Hyannis Port, the young senator smiles beside his fiancée. This was June 1953.

Happy parents three weeks before Christmas 1958.
The baby is Caroline.

Opposite: Now they are Mr. and Mrs. John F. Kennedy, following the wedding at Newport, R. I., in 1953.

The Inaugural Ball. The most notable persons applauding are Mr. and Mrs. John F. Kennedy and Mr. and Mrs. Lyndon B. Johnson.

The new First Lady of the land on way to her new home—The White House.

Wide World Photos

Above: Jacqueline takes her husband's arm as the couple attend a diplomatic reception at the White House.

Below: Caroline learns from her best teacher—her mother.

Wide World Photos

On June 21, 1962, Jacqueline Kennedy attended the opening of the White House ground-floor library, which was furnished and restored as a gift of the American Institute of Interior Designers. Reading from left: Stephen Jussel; Milton Glaser, president of A.I.D.; Mrs. Frances H. Lenygon; Jacqueline Kennedy; Mrs. Ellen L. McCluskey; and J. H. Leroy Chambers, past president of the organization.

Wide World Photos

This was the first time the Kennedy family worshiped together at St. Stephen the Martyr Roman Catholic Church in Middleburg, Va.

Wide World Photos

The President slumped down in the car just after the rifle shot. Jacqueline leaned over him as an unidentified man lends assistance.

Jacqueline Kennedy and family attend the President's funeral. Edward M. Kennedy (left); Mrs. Joseph P. Kennedy stands behind First Lady, and behind her is Sydney Lawford, daughter of Pat Kennedy. Caroline and John-John hold their mother's hands.

Left: Jacqueline Kennedy walks to her husband's grave with (left to right) Pierre Salinger, Secret Service Agent Clint Hill, and presidential aides McNall and O'Brien.

Below: On a visit to Arlington National Cemetery, John F. Kennedy, Jr., kneels beside his mother and sister Caroline.

Associated Press Photo

Wide World Photos

Jacqueline with President's brother Robert, with a model of the JFK memorabilia exhibit which will tour the United States to raise funds for the library at Harvard University.

cents to complete the two-dollar fee for admission. Mr. Dorsey happily offered him three nickels, which the Senator said he would accept as a loan. He asked for the donor's name and address, and seven days later Mr. Dorsey had a note from the Senator's wife.

"Dear Mr. Dorsey: You obviously must think us the most ungrateful couple in the world, and one that never pays its debts.

"I couldn't have been more touched by the way you lent us the money to go to the movies and neither could my husband—but when we got home we couldn't find the piece of paper he wrote your address on, and it took a week of sifting through his pockets to find it.

"Please forgive us for the long delay and thank you so much for being the kindest man in Washington on F Street last week—or in Washington—or in the U.S.A. period.

"I do hope we shall meet again soon. I wish it could be when you were trying to get into the movies and had forgotten to bring enough money so we could help you have a pleasant evening, the way you helped us."

She had signed her name and Scotch-taped three nickels to the note.

The disposal of Hickory Hill proved somewhat premature. Jacqueline was pregnant again. After the loss of the last child, when Jacqueline was so dangerously ill, that for a while it was feared she might not survive, this pregnancy was a source of both happiness and anxiety. But Caroline was born the day after Thanksgiving in 1957, and the miracle of her birth was so great that Jacqueline couldn't believe any woman had ever been so happy. Both parents found it a time of rejoicing and Jack proved himself a talented father. Men who come from large families often have a rare understanding of young children, and Jack being the second-born of his clan had felt both love and irritation for the younger brothers, Bobby and Teddy. With children, he was completely at home.

When the child was three years old, the Kennedys moved to a red brick federal house in Georgetown, of which Jacqueline has said, "I love our home in Washington. There has always been a child in it. . . . My sweet little house leans slightly to one side, and the stairs creak."

This was the house that nourished their happiness. There

was no garden in the front; the main door opened onto the walk. The backyard, however, was bricked and shaded with magnolia trees. A sense of orderliness pervaded the atmosphere.

Perhaps Jacqueline Kennedy appreciates the words of St. Augustine, who said, "Beauty is the splendor of order." For her home was always beautifully organized and she brought a kind of order into her young husband's life that rescued out of chaos his way of living. From careless clothes, baggy slacks, a pullover, he became a man of conservative fashion, whose style sense finally became a standard for masculine dress. The same spirit was brought into the house.

Jacqueline's affinity for the French style was reflected in the drawing room's fine marquetry pieces, its rare porcelains and charming and unusual bibelots. The fragile chairs with their pale-green upholstery were nevertheless designed for comfort. A bronze lion balanced Jacqueline's favorite French clock on the mantelpiece.

The dining-room carpet was splashed with red roses; the caned Louis XVI dining chairs in green and white were in perfect harmony with the pale green diamond pattern Jacqueline had painted on the floors. Her friends said with admiration that Jacqueline could always make her living as an interior decorator.

Her interest in art now included those themes that were of particular interest to her husband. A painting of distant sailboats by Eugene Boudin had been selected especially to please him. Her famous loosely arranged floral displays were often shown off to advantage in French copper cookingpots. And of course, books were everywhere, for when they were alone, both Kennedys read voraciously. Jack leaned to the works of Pitt, Fox or Burke for help in his speeches. Jacqueline was partial to the eighteenth century. As Caroline was growing up, Jacqueline often read to her of Louis XIV. Mary Van Rensselaer Thayer reported that Caroline talked of the Sun King as though he was Peter Rabbit.

In her own den on the second floor, Jacqueline kept a collection of recipes which she believed to be a necessity for a Senator's wife. Once in the first year of their marriage, Jack Kennedy invited forty guests for lunch. That would have been fine with his wife—except that he forgot to inform her of the invitation until shortly before the meal was scheduled. She managed heroically to feed them all. But after that ordeal, she was always prepared. She did much of her own shopping for fresh vegetables at local supermarkets.

She said at that time, "I'm not much of a cook, although I care terribly about food. I love to read, love to paint, love my house and my baby. I like gardening, but I'm not very good at it. I'm better at arranging flowers."

The fact that she prefers the creative aspects of managing a household doesn't detract from her painstaking attention to the details that made a home run smoothly. Her dinners, from the early years of marriage, were faultlessly planned and executed. She considers six an ideal number of guests; with more, guests have a tendency to break into islands of individual chatter, rather than participate in a warm animated give and take that gives a high polish to the art of conversation. She considers herself a "salad and cheese person," but her food has a reputation for delicacy and taste.

"I start with a good homemade soup," she once said, "then a roast, never overdone—and fresh vegetables in season. Perhaps a potato or noodle casserole. Jack loves these."

With Jacqueline to look after him, the young Senator learned to vary his taste in food and to find appetite for new dishes. He had always been a meat-and-potato man and clam chowder was a passion with him. But he soon came to appreciate *oeufs en gelée* as an appetizer and ripe mangoes for dessert.

Gone were the days when he took his lunch to the office in a brown paper bag. Jacqueline made another newsworthy contribution to her husband's well-being. It seemed to her that a man of his astonishing drive needed to replenish his energy and this was best achieved by nourishing food and ample rest. To substitute for the hot dogs, candy bars or stacked sandwiches, Jacqueline began to send hot lunches to Jack's office. These were brought to him in the same sort of hot plates that Caroline used for her meals—china plates with bottoms of nickel layers filled with hot water. The young Senator's lunches became the talk of Capitol Hill, and were perhaps an additional fillip to his genial popularity. When Jacqueline was asked why she went to such trouble when he could always eat at the Senate restaurant, she replied with the age-old wisdom of the feminine woman, "I just wanted to make sure I don't lose him."

During the week, the Kennedys usually stayed at home. Their entertaining during this period was always on a small scale. They seemed supremely happy together on their own.

But even then, Jacqueline once complained that her husband was always talking on the telephone. It seemed to her that on weekends he worked harder than ever in preparation for what was to be his successful bid for the Presidency. It was still a long-range goal, but never for a moment did he lose sight of it.

Fortunately, Jacqueline had interests to occupy her mind. One of their Georgetown neighbors was William Walton, who discussed art with Jacqueline and politics with Jack. He was later to be chosen by Jack to take charge of Jack's New York campaign.

An amusing incident involving Walton happened during Kennedy's Presidential years. Jacqueline, by then the First Lady, wrote Walton that he might expect a surprise in the mail. Lyndon B. Johnson had just presented her husband with a pregnant Hereford from his Texas ranch, and the President had quipped, "Send it to Walton. He'll know what to do with it."

Lyndon Johnson was not happy with the Presidential suggestion. "What's Walton's phone number?" he demanded. "I want to make damn sure he's there when my cow arrives!"

Caroline, whose nursery was on the third floor of the Georgetown house, rapidly proved to be following her mother's footsteps as an individualist. She had, in addition, the energy and outgoing charm of her father, whom she resembled in appearance. She had learned early the family maxim, "Kennedys don't cry."

Even in those days, Caroline was often in evidence when her father was speaking with newsmen. It fell into the natural pattern of the family life of Jacqueline's "sweet little house" to have a toddler playing at her father's feet.

Ethel Kennedy has an enormous admiration for her sister-in-law's talent for organization. "Jackie's house in Georgetown was such heaven and so supremely well organized, I always got depressed getting back to this madhouse." She was referring to her own establishment, Hickory Hill. "The wheels go round constantly in her head—you can't pigeonhole her. You have a hard time getting to the bottom of that barrel, which is great for Jack, who's so inquisitive."

Before her own marriage, Ethel, who is spritely and enormously good-natured, had been a champion horsewoman. That, and the fact that they were both married to brothers, created a deep bond between the young women.

Jack's sister Eunice, who became the wife of Sargent

Shriver, who was later given the task of organizing the Peace Corps, has said, "Jack had never done a good job of relaxing, but Jackie has gone a long way to change that."

Arthur Krock, *The New York Times*' writer, described Jacqueline as a "Victorian wife, not the chic Long Island Piping Rock variety; a Beaux Arts type of girl, merry, arch, satirical, terribly democratic, and yes, brilliant."

Naturally, not all praise for Jacqueline was so generous and gallant.

A famous international hostess made the mistake of calling the future First Lady a "beatnik." Subsequently, she was never invited to the White House during Jacqueline's tenure.

During that period of her life, Jacqueline spoke rather freely of her husband and their home in Georgetown.

". . . Jack has taught me that I must not take politics personally. He said that politics arouse the most heated emotions."

"It makes me so mad when people say Jack is not warm but cold and calculating. He loves to laugh, he is so affectionate with his daughter. She has made him so much happier. A man without a child is incomplete."

"He is a rock and I lean on him in everything. He is so kind. (Ask anyone who works for him.) And he's never irritable or sulky. He would do anything I wanted or give me anything I wanted."

"I've loved everything that's happened in our home. One of my greatest pleasures is to see that everyone else is happy in it."

"Happiness is not where you think you'll find it," *Time* Magazine reported that she said shortly after the election that brought the Presidency to her husband. "So many people poison each day by worrying about the next."

"A good wife maketh a good husband," English epigrammatist John Heywood said in 1554.

For Jacqueline, happiness and husband were synonymous.

Chapter Five

President Kennedy once said, "A man marries a woman, not a First Lady. If he becomes President, she must fit her own personality into her own concept of a First Lady's role. People do best what comes naturally."

A few months before Jacqueline found herself in that enviable predicament, she was asked how she would react if her husband were elected. "I'd be a wife and mother first," she replied, "then First Lady."

In speaking of her husband, she said with humor that had an underlying and rather poignant note of truth, "I married a whirlwind. He's indestructible. People who try to keep up with him drop like flies, including me."

This was particularly true in August 1956, when the Democratic National Convention convened to choose the Presidential candidate. Senator John F. Kennedy did not delude himself with fantasies of the Presidential nomination, but he did believe there was a chance for him to be nominated as Vice President.

His mood was optimistic. The awful humidity of Chicago didn't seem to bother him; nor even the stench of the stockyards that pervaded the city.

Although she was pregnant again, Jacqueline accompanied her husband to Chicago. She spent little time at the convention and seldom saw her husband privately. Most of the afternoons, she rested at the air-conditioned apartment of Jack's sister, Eunice Shriver.

Jack made the nominating speech for Adlai Stevenson.

As a result he had a right to hope for the Vice Presidential nomination. But despite Stevenson's good intentions, the Senator from Massachusetts lost to Kefauver. Jack was watching the convention on a TV screen in a nearby room. He managed to shrug off the disappointment. But those close to him knew how deeply he was hurt. The affable good nature that was part of his charm masked the deep anger, pain and despair that sometimes gripped him. Jack seldom met defeat, but when he did, he took it badly. Now, exhaustion brought with it an inevitable mood of depression.

Jackie, waiting it out in Eunice's home, was of little comfort to him. She herself was on the verge of despair, feeling quite shut out of his life.

Jack took off for the Riviera to work off the post-nomination melancholia at the Kennedy villa.

Jackie went to her mother's home, Hammersmith Farm, at Newport.

Jack, accompanied by his father, set off on a Mediterranean cruise.

Jackie had her second miscarriage and her life was in jeopardy.

Jack flew back to the States. He sat at her bedside, a haunted, driven man, murmuring prayers. And when her recovery was finally assured, their marriage, too, was saved. Like themselves, at various times of physical crisis, it had come through the shadow of the valley of death.

It has been said that 1956 was the turning point in both the Kennedy career and marriage.

Amusingly enough, in 1957, on Inauguration night, while Washington was celebrating President Eisenhower's second term, the young Senator and his wife attended an "Anti-Inaugural" Ball given in the Georgetown home of Mrs. Frances Lanahan. Jacqueline, in a white satin gown with Empire lines, had a marvelously carefree time. Shortly after that, the careless moments ceased. "I feel as though I had just turned into a piece of public property," she said after the election. "It's really frightening to lose your anonymity at thirty-one."

As it happened, even before the 1960 elections, the year of 1957 turned out to be one of tremendous satisfaction for both of them. For one thing, Jack's book, *Profiles in Courage,* won the Pulitzer Prize. Another fact of tremendous political encouragement: Stevenson and Kefauver were sadly beaten by Eisenhower and Nixon. The defeat which Jack had taken so much to heart turned out to be a blessing in disguise.

That was the year he told Bob Considine, the brilliant Hearst reporter who was doing a series of articles on the Kennedys: "Joe was the star of our family. He did everything better than the rest of us. If he had lived, he would have gone into politics, and he would have been elected to the House and the Senate as I was. And, like me, he would have gone out for the Vice Presidential nomination at the 1956 convention, but, unlike me, he wouldn't have been beaten. Joe would have won the nomination."

But then he'd have been defeated by Eisenhower and Nixon anyway, Jack conceded with his dry humor.

In 1960, Jack was more thoroughly equipped for the political arena. He had won the re-election for Senator from Massachusetts with a staggering plurality. His margin of victory came to 874,608 votes, which was the largest plurality ever recorded for a candidate for any office in Massachusetts.

Jacqueline took his victory with a quiet happiness.

"I'm so glad Jack comes from Massachusetts," she is reported to have said after the election. "Because it is the state with the most history. Driving from one rally to another, we'd pass John Quincy Adams's house or Harvard or Plymouth. I think I know every corner of Massachusetts. I'm glad I've had a chance to see the whole state. We spent that election night in Boston, and of course, Jack won by the most incredible majority—and we were so happy!"

Jack Kennedy had then the first inkling of a wife's role in the ultimate reach for Presidency. He said, "When we first married, my wife didn't think her role in my career would be particularly important. I was already in the Senate and she felt she could make only a limited contribution. Now, quite obviously, that I'm in a very intensive struggle—the outcome uncertain—and she plays a considerable part in it. What she does, or does not do, really affects that struggle. Since I'm completely committed, and since she is committed to me, that commits her."

Being a sensitive and perceptive person, Jacqueline was well aware of the possibility of a drastic change in her future way of life. Nevertheless, it was no doubt a relief to her to know that Jack did not want the kind of politician's wife to whom he might have to be answerable each evening. Jacqueline's way of life included seclusion and privacy, and he was reluctant to separate her from these needs. But there was no doubt in his mind nor in the minds of those close to him that it was Jacqueline who sustained him. But what did worry those close to the young Kennedys was whether Jacqueline could take the strain of another campaign. She made up her mind nevertheless that it was worth the risk, since success meant so much to her husband.

The 1960 campaign for the Presidency promised a good many obstacles for Jack. Joseph Kennedy, Jack's father, was very friendly with the late Senator Joseph McCarthy, whose very name was repugnant to Eastern liberals. Bobby Kennedy had assisted McCarthy's investigating committee, which was termed a witch hunt. There were many cruel rumors about the young Senator and his wife, gossip that old Joe Kennedy had given Jacqueline a million-dollar settlement in return for her promise not to divorce his son. A divorce for a man running for the Presidency would be disastrous. According to close friends of the couple, this story was malicious and untrue.

Among the stories passed in Republican clubs those days was a suggestion that "Jack needed less profile and more courage." Those middle-of-the-roaders who had heard of old Joe's private convictions about liberals and Jews were deeply concerned about the Senator's attitude toward civil liberties. Negroes had no faith in John F. Kennedy when it came to civil rights. Liberals remembered all too clearly his words to Paul F. Healy, printed in *The Saturday Evening Post.* "I'm not a liberal at all . . . I'm not comfortable with those people."

Jack Kennedy had a lot of growing to do, and much of his growth and tempering came after the campaign, when he was already installed in the office that encouraged statesmanship in a young man who had started out as a mere politician.

He began his campaign for the Presidency with the following statement: "For eighteen years I have been in the service of the United States, first as a naval officer in the Pacific during World War II and for the past fourteen years as a member of Congress. In the last twenty years I have traveled in nearly every continent and country—from Leningrad to Saigon, from Bucharest to Lima. From all this I have developed an image of America as fulfilling a noble and historic role as the defender of freedom in a time of maximum peril—and of the American people as confident, courageous and persevering. It is with this image that I begin this campaign."

Old Joseph Kennedy made the campaign financially possible, Bobby was enlisted as the campaign manager, and the others of the Kennedy clan contributed both time and ene
toward victory. There was a Kennedy campaig
nearly every state of the Union. The Ken
a Convair airliner, was reserved

said that the amount spent on Jack's pre-convention campaign came to about $700,000 and the total cost of the whole works put the Kennedys out perhaps $30,000,000.

Although, early in 1960, Jacqueline found herself pregnant again, she was ambivalent about her feelings. The prospect of another child was a joyous one. Yet she so wanted to share in her husband's activities. Early in the year, she did accompany Jack on several tours. She worked lovingly and tirelessly within the limits of her capacity. She devised a column called "Campaign Wife," which was mailed to Kennedy workers all through the country. She met with well-known American women to discuss the place of the intelligent woman in our culture. Even during the last months of her pregnancy (the baby was scheduled to arrive in December), she made appearances at fund-raising teas and on television.

She watched the convention from her home in Hyannis Port. As the votes for Jack piled up, her excitement mounted. But sitting in a straight-backed chair, she painted an imaginary scene of what she hoped would be her husband's triumphant return to the Cape. Her mother and stepfather sat before the television set, offering comments on the convention happenings. Shortly after midnight, the vote from the Wyoming delegates swung the nomination to Jack. At 1:50 A.M., Jack telephoned the good news to his wife. Jacqueline made a radiant appearance before the television and newsreel cameras that had been waiting for the news. Of her husband, she said simply, "He worked so hard."

Writing in *The New York Times,* September 1960, Martha Weinman commented, "When Jacqueline Kennedy, then five days the wife of the Presidential candidate, stepped aboard the family yacht in Hyannis Port, wearing an orange pullover sweater, shocking pink Capri pants and a bouffant hairdo that gamboled merrily in the breeze, even those newsmen present who could not tell shocking pink from Windsor rose, knew they were witnessing something of possible political c[illegible]ces."

[illegible]ung woman who had proudly quoted her [illegible]One woman is worth ten men" when it [illegible] "listening parties" in her house [illegible] debates. In her electioneer- [illegible]men she talked to felt [illegible] objective of every woman. Next came education, care for older people, and finally the cost of living. The budget came last.

She often quoted one of her husband's phrases in the debates: "I do not want future historians to say 'These were the years when the tide ran out for America'; I want them to say, 'These were the years when the tide came in and America started to move again.' "

This was the mother who wrote about the hurricane on the Cape that had blown off part of the roof. To Caroline's relief, the kitten, puppy and Daddy were safe—although Daddy happened to be making speeches in Texas.

This is the woman who on Columbus Day in 1960 made an appearance in New York City before a group of voters of Puerto Rican background. The streets were jammed; people were hanging out of windows and fire escapes. After Jack Kennedy concluded his pre-election appeal, he introduced his wife. "I'd like you to meet Jackie," he said.

Jackie, visibly pregnant in spite of her tentlike maternity dress, began to speak. "*Buenos dias, mis amigos . . .*" she began. Applause from the Spanish-speaking Americans was like a clap of thunder. There was no doubt among the reporters and in the mind of her husband that Jacqueline was the star of the day. The voters adored her. She continued: "Dear friends, I am so happy to be with you. My Spanish is poor but my knowledge of your history, culture and problems is better. I can assure you that if my husband is elected President you will have a real friend in the White House. Many thanks. *Viva* Kennedy."

The Republicans were quick to criticize the Kennedy exploitation of his wife's fluency in foreign languages. But Jacqueline's reply to critics gave an indication of her tact as well as her loyalty to her husband's cause. "All of these people have contributed so much to our country's culture that it seems a proper courtesy to address them in their own tongue."

Veteran reporters agreed that Jacqueline was of tremendous help to her husband in New York. This statement must have given Jacqueline enormous satisfaction, for it counteracted much of the general criticism that was beginning even to pinpoint her style and behavior.

As a result, she made a spritely defense of herself in her campaign column: "This week the doctor let me go to New York and spend two full days campaigning. I really didn't see Jack for more than a few moments alone, but at least I was part of things again. The first morning I was on Dave Garroway's show, which I enjoyed very much. In the afternoon, it was fun to pick out maternity clothes, and talking to the reporters about them was amusing. All the talk over what I wear and how I fix my hair has amused and puzzled me. What does my hairdo have to do with my husband's ability to be President?

"Actually, I've always loved clothes, and when I've had the time, I've enjoyed the universal feminine sport of shopping around from store to store and looking for new styles in the women's magazines.

"The next day I went out to the airport to meet Jack, who was late because of the crash in the morning at La Guardia. We went together to a huge luncheon at the Commodore which was very exciting. Everyone seemed so enthusiastic about Jack that I loved every minute of it. From then on we flew from one rally or reception to another and finally to a larger dinner. The next day I was back in Hyannis.

"I'll be in Washington for a few days, then back to Massachusetts to close up the house. Already everyone else has left, so I'll be glad to be back in Washington permanently after that. I hope soon to be able to go along with Jack as much as possible, particularly on trips not too far away from Washington."

This sort of warm, informal chitchat, which seemed out of character with the younger less experienced Jacqueline, certainly won for her husband the loyalty of women voters.

The hectic days that began even before her husband's nomination on the Democratic ticket increased in intensity. The Kennedys were naturally Democrats from way back. But the Bouvier and the Auchincloss clans were hidebound Republicans. Nevertheless, Hugh Auchincloss refused that year his usual annual contribution to the Republican party coffers. "I want to live in harmony with Mrs. Auchincloss and all the other members of the family," he said.

To the great surprise of the nation as a whole the problem of John F. Kennedy's religion played a small part in the campaign. There had been a tremendous sociological change in the country since 1928 when Al Smith was politically crucified for his Catholicism. Nevertheless, the campaign with its new methods of vote-getting was an exercise in endurance for the candidate's health and mental equilibrium. In the final seven days of the campaign, Jack had an average of four hours sleep a night. He ate on the fly—hot dogs, hamburgers, bowls of his favorite clam chowder. On the last day before the elections, he was aware of a sense of exhaustion worse than any he'd ever experienced. He went to the Statler Hotel in Boston, shucked his clothes and fell into a heavy sleep. In the morning, when Jacqueline arrived, they drove to cast their vote in Boston. Jack was intensely worried because Jacqueline was exposed to the jostling of the curious crowds.

Once they had voted, the young Kennedys took off by plane for Hyannis Port. They were accompanied by an entourage of reporters, photographers, aides, and the inevitable politicians. Ironically enough, Hyannis Port cast 2,783 votes that day for Kennedy and 4,515 for Nixon.

Election Day in Hyannis Port in 1960. Jack had breakfast at his father's home where the clan had gathered. He sat later on the porch of his own house, right next door, bundled in a topcoat, for the day was cold. He gave his daughter, Caroline, the gifts he had brought home from the campaign.

He talked briefly before lunch to his father. He went later to his brother Bobby's house, where they listened to nationwide reports coming in from key centers. Louis Harris, a well-known public-opinion analyst, was installed in an upstairs bedroom, busily interpreting reports and trends. During the afternoon, Harris's reports were somewhat depressing. It seemed that voters from Kentucky, which Kennedy had been counting on, had gone for the great part to Nixon. Only the big cities seemed to be loyal to Kennedy.

During dinner that evening, nevertheless, Jack seemed to maintain his calm. Or perhaps, as some friends suggested, weariness had left him detached. Dinner in his Hyannis Port cottage was shared with Jacqueline and their good friend, the artist, William Walton. Later, Ted Sorensen joined the trio, and as the reports grew more encouraging, Jacqueline and the others were elated. Only Jack retained his realistic point of view. He was still worried about the Southwest and the South itself. The news grew more disturbing, but he persuaded his wife to go to bed about 11:30 without letting her in on his feeling of anxiety. When Jack went to bed at 3:40 A.M. the election results were still up in the air.

Finally, at 5:35 A.M., news was flashed across the television screens. It seemed to be Kennedy for President by a narrow margin. By 9:30 in the morning, when Jack awoke and was still in bed, the news came that California had gone for him.

It was official now. John Fitzgerald Kennedy was the next President of the United States.

While the President-elect was watching Herbert Klein, Nixon's representative, over television, there was a sudden hush from the group in the living room as Klein conceded Nixon's defeat.

Afterward, the new President-elect asked a question that was to become habitual with him whenever his wife was out of the room: "Where's Jackie?"

She was walking on the beach, a solitary figure in an old raincoat, a kerchief bound around her head, her figure heavy with her pregnancy. Jack brought her back to the house and they all dressed for the formal family portrait. The rest of the day was spent, in happiness and victory, at the Kennedy compound.

But later in the evening, while films were shown at his father's house, Jack slipped away to be alone. The margin of his victory was too slight to bring a man of his ambitious drive complete fulfillment. He had a prescience that his task to unite the country would be a formidable one.

The new baby was due on Christmas. A Caesarian section would be necessary—Jacqueline's third. It was therefore considered unwise for her to attempt the trip South, so Jack went alone to Palm Beach. He was bone weary after the campaign and she felt a rest was essential for him.

Jack, however, flew back to Washington to be with her and Caroline for Thanksgiving dinner. The William Waltons were their guests, and Mr. Walton later reported that Jacqueline had never looked more beautiful. Dinner over, Jack took a flight back to Palm Beach.

Shortly after ten that evening, Jacqueline began to hemorrhage. Her obstetrician, Dr. John W. Walsh, arrived swiftly and made arrangements for her to be taken by ambulance to the Georgetown Hospital, a mile and a half away. Jackie was terrified of losing the child, but Dr. Walsh gave her the confidence that perhaps he himself did not feel.

When the President-elect's private plane landed in Palm Beach, he was told of the emergency. Twenty minutes later, he was on his way North again, and while he was traveling toward his wife's bedside, pale and shaken, the news came over the radio that Jacqueline had given birth to a boy, and that both mother and baby were doing well.

From the Washington airport, he sped to the hospital,

dashed up the stairs and raced into his wife's room. He was a proud and happy father. The baby, he later told the press, was to be named John F. Kennedy, Jr.

"It was really something, wasn't it?" he said with his wide smile.

John-John, as his indulgent father was to call him, was born a month prematurely on November 25th.

Although during the campaign she was wearing maternity clothes, John-John's mother made fashion history. She was included in the world's best-dressed women in New York Couture Group's international poll of 2,000 fashion experts.

Inauguration Day, January 20, 1961, was ushered in by a blizzard. Icy winds blew up to thirty-two miles an hour; eight inches of snow had fallen and all night long thousands of workmen with trucks and snowplows had labored to clear Pennsylvania Avenue from the White House to the Capitol for the Inaugural parade.

Some of the most important dignitaries were unable to attend because of the storm. Former President Herbert Hoover's plane was unable to land. However, a former First Lady, Mrs. Woodrow Wilson (who was Edith Bolling Galt), braved the elements to make the last public appearance before her death on December 28, 1961.

The Democrats, celebrating their return to executive power, refused to curtail any plans for the big parade of bands, representatives of the armed forces, floats from the various states, and even a Navy PT boat in honor of Kennedy's wartime heroism.

Despite the 20-degree cold, hundreds of bundled up spectators gathered along the route and dense crowds thronged at the Capitol, traditional scene of the swearing-in ceremony.

President-elect Kennedy, at forty-three the youngest man ever to attain America's highest office, and the first Roman Catholic to do so, had begun the day by attending Mass.

At 11:30 A.M., with Jacqueline, who was wearing a beige coat and round sable collar, he arrived at the north portico of the White House, where they were met by the outgoing President and his wife. It was typical of the thoughtful Eisenhowers that they made the young Kennedys drink hot coffee before proceeding in the freezing weather.

By contrast to his successor, Eisenhower was the oldest

man ever to serve as President. Together, they now rode to the Capitol where they were greeted by the Marine Corps Band playing "Hail to the Chief."

At the Capitol, Jacqueline, the third-youngest First Lady, smiled warmly and proudly as her husband was sworn in. Tears streamed down the cheeks of Ethel Kennedy as her brother-in-law's hand rested upon the Bible that had been in his mother's family for generations. Richard Nixon stood smiling stoically, during the changeover, and Jacqueline sought out Mrs. Nixon and talked with her. Also on the podium were Mamie Eisenhower and Lady Bird Johnson. Former President Harry S Truman was very much in evidence. Eleanor Roosevelt with her usual grace remarked of Jacqueline: "I know she'll do very well."

One wonders whether, at this supreme moment in her life, Jacqueline Kennedy recalled the time when, covering President Eisenhower's inauguration, she had observed in her news story that "Mamie's lively laughter could be heard far back in the crowd . . . while Mrs. Truman sat stolidly with her gaze glued on the blimp overhead through most of the ceremony."

She also wrote that "Ike planted a kiss on Mamie's cheek right after taking the oath." When President Kennedy failed to follow suit by kissing his wife, many American women were volubly disappointed. However, Kennedy's strict New England upbringing just didn't allow kissing in public. Jacqueline, however, did give her husband a chuck under the chin.

President Kennedy's voice was strong and steady as he read the Inaugural address that contained this memorable passage:

"And so, my fellow Americans, ask not what your country can do for you—ask what you can do for your country. My fellow citizens of the world, ask not what America will do for you, but what together we can do for the freedom of man. Let every nation know, whether it wish us well or ill, that we shall pay any price, bear any burden, meet any hardship, support any friend or oppose any foe in order to assure the survival and success of liberty."

The luncheon was held in the Capitol after the inauguration and was somewhat hurried, as events were running forty-five minutes behind schedule.

Afterward, President and Mrs. Kennedy returned from the swearing-in ceremony in the White House bubble-top car from which even the transparent top had been removed.

Then, from a reviewing stand set up in front of the White House, they watched the great procession wind past.

In view of the weather, some of the floats did seem rather unseasonable; the one from Florida had girls perched among palm trees, and orchid scent was blown on the arctic air from a gadget on the Hawaii float.

It was 3:27 P.M. before young Mrs. Kennedy, after standing several hours in the bitter cold, left the reviewing box to rest before attending five Inaugural balls that evening.

Wearing a stunning gown of her own design, Jacqueline Kennedy was the New Frontier's brightest star and her husband liked it that way. Now placed permanently among the Smithsonian Institution's collection of First Ladies' gowns, Jacqueline's dress was of white peau d'ange with a bodice embroidered in silver. A white chiffon overblouse gave it an almost ethereal, misty effect.

The President's mother was wearing a gown she had first worn to the Court of St. James in London when her husband was American Ambassador. Mrs. Joseph Kennedy had still retained her faultless figure.

Starting out at Washington's Inaugural Ball at the Mayflower Hotel, President and Mrs. Kennedy planned to visit the other four; but after three parties, Jacqueline, still convalescing after John-John's difficult birth, was obliged to go home to bed.

So crowded were the affairs that both President Kennedy and Vice President Lyndon B. Johnson expressed unfulfilled ambitions "to see someone dance."

An editorial in the Charleston, S.C., *Evening Post* aptly summed up the evening:

> Let all of us who sit before the fireside tonight murmur a word of thanks that circumstances have allowed us to be some place other than Washington.
>
> The national capital is a hotbed of madness this evening; what with thousands of persons jammed like sardines at five or more inaugural balls, which climax a full day of parading, cocktailing, handshaking, pushing and shoving, all of which have come to be a part of the swearing-in of a new President of the United States.
>
> What the new top executive and his wife and his top aides have had to endure since the sun first shone on the Potomac this day is enough to make strong men blanch.

It was irony that the young woman who shied away from

publicity, who had always been what her friends called an introspective "private" person should suddenly be subjected to the most harsh, critical spotlight ever turned on any woman. True, she had experienced an inkling of it during the pre-election campaign. But after becoming the First Lady, she found the avalanche of bouquets and brickbats almost too much to cope with.

In spite of the fact that Tish Baldridge, her old Vassar College friend who became her social secretary, said, "Jacqueline Kennedy is the woman who has everything—including the President of the United States," the First Lady was very vulnerable to criticism in the early months of her husband's tenure.

During the frenetic campaign days, Jacqueline and Jack had so little time together that she was often pitied for living out her lonely pregnancy. This is an emotionally trying time for any woman, and her husband's love, loyalty and presence are necessary to sustain her. But while she was nourished by her husband's love and loyalty, his physical absence was a sore trial to her. Even before they could spend time getting reacquainted, the obligations of the White House descended on them, and with it the merciless glare of publicity.

Fortunately, Jacqueline discovered that the apex of her husband's career was the magic that drew them closer together and cemented the basic strength and devotion that was mutually important to them. However, Jacqueline was soon to say rather sadly, "It is terrifying to lose your identity. . . ."

Although the President's wife is obliged to create an identity of her own, it must, through years of tradition, conform to that which the country expects of a First Lady. Mrs. Herbert Hoover, Mrs. Bess Truman, Mrs. Franklin Roosevelt, Mrs. Mamie Eisenhower, filled the outlines perfectly. But here in the newest First Lady was youth, beauty, a culture familiar perhaps only to a small percentage of the country, an affinity for French language and elegance, and a complete insouciance where clothes were concerned. Here was an individualist who would remain, no matter what her position, completely and uniquely herself.

Jacqueline's style sense, her impeccable and elegant taste in interior decoration, her love of horses and the arts, all were a little intimidating to the average American housewife. Nevertheless, Jacqueline armed herself with a social and press secretary, both young women of equal glamor, and the processing of a new kind of First Lady began.

The impression Jacqueline made from the Inaugural Day created a lasting and somewhat shattering impression on American style and cultural tastes. Although the January day was bitterly cold and many women of high station were swathed in furs, the First Lady was clad in a beige woolen coat of the classic simplicity that was to become her trademark. It was only two months since the Caesarian birth of her son, John-John, yet she withstood the rigors of the bitter climate, the endless parades and the gala evening with remarkable and charming endurance that courteously hid from the eyes of the world whatever weariness she may have suffered.

A few months before the election, models who bore a resemblance to Jacqueline Kennedy—wide eyes, leonine haircut, square face with a full lower lip—were a drug on the market. The day after the Inauguration, they were plied with modeling jobs. Overnight, the "Jackie" look was In. Even store manikins had faces fashioned like hers.

The new First Lady had designed her ball gown for the evening of the Inauguration. Years of attention to the styles particularly suited to her long slim body had taught her the little tricks by which the smart young woman collaborates with her dressmaker. Mini Rhea, the brilliant little dressmaker who in earlier years helped Jacqueline to discover her most suitable style, had inspired the young woman with the importance of perfect fit, the couturier tricks of letting out a little here, adding darts to give roundness and allure to the bosom.

The gala that Frank Sinatra planned in honor of the Kennedys was two hours late in starting, but the Kennedy clan remained with it until after midnight. Jacqueline, exhausted, had slipped away earlier, but the rest of the party went on to Paul Young's restaurant for a special party given by the President's father. The first night of his Presidency, Jack Kennedy didn't get away from well-wishers until four in the morning. Secret Service agents bade him good night. He walked tall and erect into the front door of the White House. A new family had moved in.

"She's going to be a supersonic First Lady," predicted a leading Republican. He was right. Jacqueline Kennedy would compare favorably with her predecessors in the White House. Blessed with a gift for graceful living, she came in time to enjoy her role as the President's wife.

There were changes in the feminine obligations of the

White House. A French chef was installed, for Mrs. Kennedy has a gourmet's appreciation of fine food, and her taste had rubbed off on her husband's palate. They both drank sparingly but enjoyed a daiquiri before dinner. It took the husband of one of the best dressed women in the world to make the old-fashioned rocking chair fashionable. And overnight, the fragile delicacy of the Empire period became chic. America tossed out Swedish and Danish modern and combed shops for lovely old French and English pieces, delicate porcelain cups and saucers to use for cigarettes and ash trays. Attractive women who had parked their brains suddenly felt safe in airing them in public. Vaughn Meader's record album, "The First Family," won a gold record for having sold over a million copies. The Kennedys were young, elegant, cultured—and not only an American ideal but the idol of the world.

There were some criticisms, naturally. There had never been a First Lady like Jacqueline Kennedy. But she made the White House a home whose hospitality their guests could enjoy and both the press and VIP's made the comment that entertainment at the White House had never been informal and relaxed and "fun."

Martha Dandridge Custis Washington (1731-1802), who never actually occupied the White House since it was not completed during her husband's administration, had this to say when she ceased to be First Lady: "I have felt more like a prisoner than anything else." In common with Jacqueline Kennedy, she was a meticulous housekeeper and a tower of strength to her husband. Of his grandmother, George Washington Parke Custis later was to write:

"Mrs. Washington was remarkable for her affable and dignified manners, and her courteous and kindly demeanor to all who approached her. Again it is notorious that the politicians and statesmen of both parties were equally well and kindly received at the Presidential mansion. . . . In the whole period of the first Presidency, I never heard Mrs. Washington engage in any political controversy, or, indeed, touch on the subject of politics at all."

Unlike Jacqueline, Martha Washington was not the star of her husband's Inaugural Ball, held in New York on May 7, 1789. She did not arrive in the city until the end of the month. The country did not furnish the President's House, either in New York City or Philadelphia, both at various times the seat of government. The President had to furnish his own home.

Washington, like President Kennedy, was content to leave household affairs to his wife. "Furnish Mrs. Washington with what money she may want and from time to time ask her if she does want, as she is not fond of applying," he instructed his aide, Lear. Once, when Washington was writing his agent to sell some tobacco in Virginia, he praised his wife's excellent memory, saying that it ". . . rarely occurs to me, except when I am reminded of it by Mrs. Washington."

Home at last in Mount Vernon, her public life over as wife of the President, Martha Washington, or Lady Washington as she was commonly known, wrote Lucy Knox, wife of General Henry Knox, the first Secretary of War:

"I cannot tell you, my dear friend, how much I enjoy home after having been deprived of one so long, for our dwelling in New York and Philadelphia was not home, only a sojourning. The General and I feel like children just released from school or from a hard taskmaster . . ."

Of Mrs. John Adams (1744-1818), wife of the second Chief Executive, former President Harry S Truman with typical candor said: "She would have made a better President than her husband."

Unfortunately, New Englander Abigail Smith Adams was born at a time when it was believed that women, like children, "should be seen and not heard." Although self-taught, she was one of America's most brilliant First Ladies. Abigail, as a President's wife, was the first to live in the newly built White House.

With a frankness matching Mr. Truman's, she wrote her daughter:

Washington,
21 November, 1800

My dear child:

I arrived here on Sunday last, and without meeting with any accident worth noticing, except losing ourselves when we left Baltimore, and going eight or nine miles on the Frederick Road, by which means we were obliged to go the other eight through wood, where we wandered two hours without finding a guide, or the path. . . . The house is made habitable, but there is not a single apartment finished, and all within-side, except the plastering, has been done since Briesler came. We have not the least fence, yard, or other convenience, without, and the great unfinished audience room [now the

East Room] I make a drying-room of, to hang up the clothes in. The principal stairs are not up, and will not be this winter. . . .

Affectionately your mother,
A. Adams

As Jacqueline Kennedy applied her energy to restoring the White House for posterity, so Abigail Adams used her energy in a series of letters, each paragraph a historian's delight. Once in the White House, Abigail's husband, the second President, complained that she sat at her writing desk so long during their brief private hours together that being with her did him no good. His loss was our gain, for Abigail was gifted with rare powers of observation. However, as her daughter put it, Mrs. Adams's great love was "a dish of politics." One of the charges made against her husband when he sought reelection was that his wife had "a degree of influence over the public conduct of her husband." It helped to defeat him.

A progressive for her times, Abigail Adams wrote her husband when he was among the Massachusetts delegation to the Continental Congress: "I wish most sincerely there was not a slave in the province. It always seemed a most iniquitous scheme to me to fight ourselves for what we are robbing the Negroes of, who have as good a right to freedom as we have."

Adams proudly showed this and other letters of hers to fellow delegates.

At the White House, Abigail maintained the same strict etiquette as her friend Martha Washington had done at the President's House in Philadelphia. Concerning her role as First Lady, she declared: "I shall esteem myself peculiarly fortunate, if at the cost of my public life, I can retire esteemed, beloved and equally respected with my predecessor."

In her time, the entire Congress was required to call upon the new President. In the sparsely furnished White House this must have created a problem. Upon leaving for good, she said somewhat imperiously: "I leave to posterity to reflect upon the times past; and I leave them characters to contemplate."

Her son, John Quincy Adams, was to become President in his own right.

Believing that the young republic needed more social graces, Dorothea Payne Todd Madison (1768-1849), better known as "Dolley," made it her business to see that they were acquired. The wife of James Madison, fourth President, loved to give parties which were sensational. Although at his inauguration her husband was the first Chief Executive whose entire costume was made in the United States, Dolley went farther afield for her own apparel. At a fabulous White House reception held New Year's Day, 1814, she stood resplendent in a pink satin gown lined with ermine, imported from France. On her head was the latest plumed turban, fashioned of white velvet and satin. Dolley dwarfed the President, who was three inches shorter than she was and, though twenty years her husband's junior, she liked to call him "my darling little husband."

During the Madisons' residence, the White House witnessed its first wedding. Dolley's sister, Mrs. Lucy Payne Washington, widow of George Steptoe Washington, married Justice Thomas Todd of the United States Supreme Court. All her life, Dolley was something of a matchmaker.

She was also a fashion setter, and just as Jacqueline Kennedy started the rage for bouffant hair styles, so did Dolley Madison become, as painter William Dunlap noted, "the leader of everything fashionable in Washington." When she bought an exotic macaw, other women followed suit; and her habit of snuff-taking was quickly copied, though Aaron Burr deplored it.

Political friends and foes of her husband were equally welcome at the White House. She expected them all to behave like civilized human beings. Their wives, after her husband became President, called her "Lady Presidentess" or "Her Majesty." When Mrs. Anthony Merry, wife of the British minister, complained that Dolley's well-stocked table was "more like a harvest home supper than the entertainment of a Secretary of State," Dolley serenely replied: "The profusion of my table, so repugnant to foreign customs, arises from the happy circumstances of abundance and prosperity in our country."

Like Mrs. Kennedy, she truly loved the White House. She spent about $11,000 supplied by the government upon new decorations. Her purchase included a guitar and a piano, both indispensable aids in entertaining.

A lover of books which she found better as conversation pieces than for actual reading, Dolley would "sail" into a reception, volume in hand. And, as might be expected, it was she who instituted the first inaugural ball at the White House.

Her marriage to James Madison had been approved of by her distant cousin, Martha Washington, who advised: "He will make thee a good husband, and all the better for being so much older. We both approved of it: the esteem and friendship existing between Mr. Madison and my husband is very great, and we would wish thee to be happy."

"Queen Dolley," another of her contemporaries' nicknames for her, liked to send to France for her gowns, yet on mornings in her own home before coming to Washington, she continued to wear a Quaker wife's white apron and gray gown.

Dolley's finest hour came in 1812 when war with Britain was declared. When her husband left the White House to take personal command of Commodore Joshua Barney's battery near Bladensburg, Maryland, telling her to take care of herself and the Cabinet papers, she replied that she "had no fear but for him, and the success of our army." The guard left to protect her and the White House disappeared, some to join the army, others to seek their own safety. Jean Pierre Sioussant, her steward, was given the task of finding safe quarters for Dolley's pet macaw. The bird survived the invasion and is one of the earliest pets recorded as belonging to a First Family.

On August 23, 1814, she calmly wrote her sister, Lucy:

Dear Sister:

My husband left me yesterday morning to join General Winder. He inquired anxiously whether I had courage, or firmness to remain in the President's House until his return on the morrow or succeeding day. . . . He desires I should be ready at a moment's warning to enter my carriage and leave the city. . . . I am accordingly ready; I have pressed as many Cabinet papers into trunks as to fill one carriage; our private property must be sacrificed. . . . I am determined not to go myself until I see Mr. Madison safe, and he can accompany me, as I hear of much hostility towards him. Disaffection stalks around us. My friends and acquaintances are all gone. . . .

Next day, August 24, the President still had not returned. Climbing to the White House roof, Dolley viewed through her spyglass defeat instead of victory, with disillusioned American soldiers scattering in all directions. At three in the afternoon she again wrote her sister:

Will you believe it, my sister? We have had a battle, or skirmish near Bladensburg, and I am still here within sound of the cannon! Mr. Madison comes not; may God protect him! Two messengers, covered with dust, come to bid me fly, but here I mean to wait for him. . . . At this late hour, a wagon has been procured; I have had it filled with the plate and most valuable portable articles belonging to the house; whether it will reach its destination, the Bank of Maryland . . . events must determine.

Our kind friend, Mr. [Charles] Carroll, has come to hasten my departure, and is in very bad humor with me because I insist on waiting until the large painting of General Washington is secured, and it requires to be unscrewed from the wall. This process was found to be too tedious for these perilous moments; I have ordered the frame to be broken, and the canvas taken out; it is done, and the precious portrait placed in the hands of two gentlemen of New York for safe keeping. And now, dear sister, I must leave this house, or the retreating army will make me a prisoner in it, by filling up the road I am directed to take. When I shall again write to you, or where I shall be tomorrow, I cannot tell!

The famous painting by Gilbert Stuart, acquired by the White House in 1800, was saved by her prompt action and today it is the only object from President Adams's administration to survive there.

Dolley commented: "I acted thus because of my respect for General Washington, not that I felt a desire to gain laurels."

Escaping with Sukey, her maid, in a carriage when the British were already burning Washington's public buildings, Mrs. Madison finally reached the safety of a soldier's encampment to the north of Georgetown. She was refused hospitality at a tavern by an irate woman who screamed, "Your husband has got mine out fighting, and damn you, you shan't stay in my house."

Three days later, Dolley returned with the President to the blackened shell of the White House. "I cannot tell you," she said, "what I felt on re-entering it, such destruction, such confusion. The fleet in full view and in the act of robbing Alexandria. The citizens expecting another visit—and at night, the rockets were seen flying near us."

When Philadelphia invited the United States government to move back again, it was Dolley who persuaded her husband otherwise. She thought that the nation's capital should remain Washington where the Founding Fathers had wanted it, but she never again lived in the White House during her husband's administration. It was not made habitable again until President Monroe's time.

After Madison's death in 1835, his widow lived at Montpelier where she was as hospitable to guests as she had been in the White House. The tribute paid her by a leading woman writer at this period might well have been written for Jacqueline Kennedy:

"She is a strong-minded woman, fully capable of entering into her husband's occupations and cares; and there is little doubt that he owed much to her intellectual companionship, as well as to her ability in sustaining the outward dignity of his office."

In her retirement she became the confidante of Presidents. The widower, President Martin Van Buren, asked her advice concerning the marital future of his son, Abraham. Dolley thoughtfully suggested the beautiful South Carolinian, Angelica Singleton, one of her relatives, as a suitable wife, and Abraham promptly married the young lady, whose portrait by the New York artist, Henry Inman, is today one of the finest in the White House collection.

On July 12, 1849, death came to Dolley Madison. Her funeral was as elaborate as any Chief Executive's, and the twelfth President, Zachary Taylor, was among the mourners.

Vice President John Tyler, who became President upon the death of William Henry Harrison, April 4, 1841, was responsible for bringing two beautiful young ladies to the White House. His first wife, Letitia Christian Tyler, was still suffering from the effects of a paralytic attack so she was unable to act as mistress of the White House. Therefore Elizabeth Priscilla Cooper Tyler, wife of his eldest son, Robert, became acting First Lady. Better known as Priscilla Cooper, she was the daughter of the English actor, Thomas A. Cooper, and his American wife, Mary Fairlie Cooper. Perhaps the most famous performance she ever gave was at Charleston, South Carolina. The play was entitled *The Honey Moon* and Priscilla found much competition in a member of the audience who preferred the sound of the trombone to her acting. He was Osceola, the Seminole Indian, then a prisoner of war, and the audience had attended the performance as much to see him wearing his ceremonial regalia as to watch the play.

Priscilla—as Mrs. Robert Tyler—left this poignant note concerning her White House days:

"My first state dinner is over; oh, such a long one, our first dinner in the State Dining Room. I was the only lady present at the table. I tried to be as cheerful as possible, though I felt miserable all the time, as my baby was crying, and I received message after message to come to the nursery."

Letitia Tyler died September 10, 1842. She was the first President's wife to die while her husband was still in office. President Tyler soon remarried . . . the first President to marry while serving in that capacity. His bride was the young, beautiful, intellectual Julia Gardiner, known as "the Rose of Long Island." The marriage was much criticized, not only by the American people, but by Tyler's own children, some of whom were older than the bride. Tyler was fifty-four, his bride twenty-four. They were married June 26, 1844, at the Church of the Ascension, New York City, and five boys and two girls were born of the union. Young Mrs. Tyler enjoyed her short eight months' sojourn in the Executive Mansion where, according to *The White House; An Historic Guide,* published in 1963, she changed her husband's "simple style of country living" and "established an extremely regal style." They were accused of "living in a style far too lavish for their position."

Although an invalid when her husband, Millard Fillmore, succeeded to the Presidency, Abigail Powers Fillmore (1798-1853), a former schoolteacher, established the first White House library in the second-floor Oval Room. She could relax there in comfort with her beloved books and piano. As mentioned earlier, Jacqueline Kennedy also took a keen interest in the library.

Abigail's daughter, Mary Abigail Fillmore, assumed the functions of First Lady for her mother. The studious Abigail died less than a month after her husband ended his term of office, ironically having contracted a chill while attending the inauguration of President Franklin Pierce.

When Jacqueline Kennedy first came to live in the White House she remarked, "Jefferson is the President with whom I have the most affinity. But Lincoln is the one I love." It was to the Lincoln Room she would escape for a few quiet moments where she said, "It gave me great comfort . . . to touch something I knew he had touched was a real link with him. The kind of peace I felt in that room was what you feel when going to church."

But Mary Todd Lincoln (1818-1882), surely the most tragic occupant of the White House, found little peace there.

Criticized by her enemies on account of what they termed her "wild extravagances, gaucherie and insane jealousy," she was even so, a compassionate woman. When, in 1861, she heard that a young soldier, William Scott, was to be shot for falling asleep on picket duty, she "grew so nervous" that the President actually told General McClellan that "the Lady President" greatly hoped the man would be pardoned, and he was.

When Willie (William Wallace Lincoln), the eleven-year-old son, died February 20, 1862, of typhoid fever, Lincoln for the most part was able to control his outward expressions of sorrow, but his wife could not. Her grief for the blue-eyed youngster could only find an outlet in sudden outbursts of hysteria and weeping, and Elizabeth Keckley, the Negro mantua-maker who was the First Lady's dressmaker, said that Mrs. Lincoln was never able to look at Willie's picture or ever again enter the bedroom where he died. Mrs. Keckley had once seen Mr. Lincoln lead his prostrate wife to the window, where, pointing toward the grim battlements of a sanitorium, he said in a kindly voice, "Mother, do you see that large white building on the hill yonder? Try and control your grief, or it will drive you mad, and we may have to send you there."

Extremely possessive, Mrs. Lincoln once told Adam Badeau, military secretary to General Grant: "Do you know, sir, that I never permit the President to see any woman alone?" Yet apparently she had no objection to Vinnie Ream, a poor seventeen-year-old Wisconsin girl, who came to the White House to model Lincoln's head in clay. (Vinnie was later to become the first woman to receive a commission from Congress to make the statue of Lincoln that now stands in the Rotunda of the Capitol.)

Mrs. Lincoln was in her forties and pleasantly plump during her "reign" at the White House. She was hard on photographers, and once ordered Civil War photographer Mathew Brady to destroy all the negatives he had ever made of her.

Since she was a Southerner married to the President of the United States, there were many during the war who questioned her patriotism and loyalty. One of her brothers, George Rogers Clark Todd, was a surgeon with the Confederate army. Her half brother, Samuel Briggs Todd, a Confederate soldier, was killed at the Battle of Shiloh; another half brother, David H. Todd, died of wounds received at Vicksburg; and yet another, her beloved red-headed Alexander H. Todd, lost his life at Baton Rouge, Louisiana.

Mrs. Lincoln was another lady who liked to see only the finest furnishings in the President's House and she often petitioned Congress for money to help with her grandiose plans.

Lincoln told Emilie Helm, the widow of a Confederate who was invited to stay in the White House: "I feel worried about Mary, her nerves have gone to pieecs; she cannot hide from me that the strain she has been under has been too much for her mental as well as her physical health." He also worried about the cruel "stabs given Mary" by the newspapers.

She was often plagued with headaches. Yet when she felt well Mary Todd Lincoln tried to lighten her husband's burden. Mrs. Keckley told the story of how a downcast Lincoln had entered the room to be asked by his wife: "Is there any news?"

"Yes, plenty of news, but no good news," he replied. "It is dark, dark everywhere." He picked up the Bible and read aloud while Mrs. Lincoln sat quietly knitting by his side.

On April 14, 1865, the Lincolns attended Ford's Theatre with their eldest son, Robert, home from the Union Army. The play was a new comedy by Tom Taylor, entitled *Our American Cousin*. During the performance, a little after ten in the evening, the President was shot in the back of the head by John Wilkes Booth. Mortally wounded, he was carried across the street to William Peterson's boardinghouse, and at twenty-one minutes, fifty-five seconds past seven the next morning, Abraham Lincoln, sixteenth President of the United States, was dead.

Rain fell on Mary Todd Lincoln's head as she was led to a carriage. Upon seeing the theater, scene of the tragedy, she screamed hysterically, "Oh, that dreadful house! That dreadful house!"

Lincoln lay in state in the East Room of the White House. The mirrors were veiled, the rich crimson damask drapes camouflaged with black.

Mary Todd Lincoln never fully recovered from her husband's death. Upon leaving the White House she became a tragic, misunderstood figure. Crucified again by the press for trying to sell her White House gowns to pay her debts, she fled to Europe, where for six years she lived in second-rate hotels and lodging houses. To Vinnie Ream, the little sculptress, she wrote of "my heart *then* as *now,* filled with unutterable love for him who so truly and fervently returned it."

Upon her return to America in October 1880, the New York *Sun* recorded the following:

When the *Amerique* reached New York, a throng was assembled on the dock and a greater throng was in the street outside the gates. During the tedious process of working the ship into her dock, there was a great crush in that part of the vessel where the gangplank was to be swung. Among the passengers who were here gathered was an aged lady; she was dressed plainly; her face was furrowed and her hair was streaked with white—this was the widow of Abraham Lincoln. She was almost unnoticed. She came alone across the ocean, but a nephew met her at Quarantine. She had spent the last four years in the south of France.

When the gangplank was swung aboard, Madame [Sarah] Bernhardt and her companions, including Madame Colombier, of the troupe, were the first to descend. The fellow voyagers of the actress pressed about her to bid her adieu, and a cheer was raised, which turned her head and provoked an astonished smile as she stepped upon the wharf. The gates were besieged, and there was some difficulty in bringing the carriage, which was to convey the actress to the hotel. She temporarily waited in the freight office at the entrance to the wharf.

Mrs. Lincoln, leaning upon the arm of her nephew, walked toward the gate. A policeman touched the aged lady on the shoulder and bade her stand back. She retreated with her nephew into the line of spectators, while Manager Abbey's carriage was slowly brought in. Madame Bernhardt was handed in, and the carriage made its way through a mass of struggling longshoremen and idlers who pressed about it and stared into the open window. After it went out the others, who had been passengers on the *Amerique,* Mrs. Lincoln with the rest.

In another time, another place, a continuity writer for a radio station in Columbus, Ohio, said, "Everyone has to have a real hero just once. Kennedy's mine, and I think his wife is the greatest thing we've had in the White House for years. She'll be a wonderful First Lady—maybe even another Eleanor Roosevelt."

But because of her husband's martyrdom, Jacqueline Kennedy has since been likened to Mary Todd Lincoln.

Chapter Six

Among the most endearing photographs of the First Family were those by Mark Shaw, taken on the shore near Hyannis Port. One in particular shows a young father, clad in slacks and knit jersey, lying on his back on the damp sand and holding his young daughter in his arms above him, while the child's mother, in Capri pants and a loose shirt, watches both affectionately. It is a reflection of the most touching felicity and once again reveals a side of the President reserved mainly for young children.

Caroline, the child, in a striped bathing suit, is obviously ecstatic with delight.

The embrace of a child is a form of wordless communication that Jacqueline Kennedy well understands. The part of herself that has a warm affinity for the young, that understands and suffers and rejoices with them, can join in this tender, significant communication.

Her children are aware of this gift.

A child feels his first contact with the world through his mother's arms. Her embrace is his world. Moods of tension and anxiety in the mother will create similar reactions within the child and as a result, his later adjustment to the world of his peers may be difficult.

The Kennedy children have blossomed under their mother's unaffected emotional communication with them. They have a radiant model on which to pattern themselves. Children grow only in the mold of those who deeply influence them.

Children also adore the unexpected, the surprise, the little shared secrets. On this nourishment, the young ego grows strong and healthy. The little girl who is her daddy's best girl, the little boy who loves his mother but admires his father are destined to have an easier emotional time in life than those who cannot, through whatever circumstances, make that initial adjustment.

The love of both parents has given Caroline and John-John a strong cushion of warmth and security. You have only to see the picture of the family leaving church services on a Sunday morning—Caroline holding the hand of her father, John-John in his mother's arms—to know this is a warm, united family.

Just as her own mother taught Jacqueline to ride a horse early, so the First Lady has initiated Caroline into the world of horseflesh. There are photographs of Jacqueline driving a pony cart, the baby boy on her lap and the little girl beside her. Or Jacqueline on her spirited horse, with John-John sharing the saddle with his mother; or Jacqueline wheeling the baby in his carriage around the White House grounds, with Caroline in overalls sturdily tagging after her. The older generation might criticize this informality, but young mothers over the country were entranced.

Whenever possible, Mrs. Kennedy has spent time with her children, although they have always been in the care of nurses. She is not one to look after them in the same practical daily routine that Rose Kennedy cared for her brood. Caroline daubs when her mother is painting. No doubt the little girl will be bilingual early, for in the family home there are many foreign language records.

When Sander Vanocur of NBC asked Mrs. Kennedy how she brought up her children, she answered, "I always imagined I'd raise my children completely on my own. But once you have them, you find you need help. So I do need Dr. Spock a lot and I find it such a relief to know that other people's children are as bad as yours at the same age."

To raise children in the White House would seem an insurmountable task for parents dedicated to bringing up normal well-adjusted moppets. But to raise a child like Caroline, with her enormous friendliness and curiosity, in a world of reporters, cameramen and photographers, was for Mrs. Kennedy a losing battle.

Indeed, the precocious, enchanting Caroline was such a headline grabber that a woman member of the Republican National Committee remarked, "There ought to be a law against lady politicians who are three years old."

Caroline, riding her tricycle in the White House corridors; Caroline engaging VIP's in her own enchanting level of conversation; Caroline chasing her hamsters who had got out of their cages became one of the Kennedys' most engaging public relations ploys.

Mrs. Kennedy was considerably disturbed by all this publicity about her children, but the President found it vastly amusing. The White House employees are supposed to sign pledges that bind them to secrecy about the activities of the Presidential family. The President often remarked it was working well, except for Caroline. He said, "She keeps wanting to hold press conferences."

Nevertheless, the high spot of the President's grueling day was often a visit from his children. The fact that Caroline once interrupted a news conference by toddling into the room wearing her mother's slippers did not disturb him. Perhaps he knew that this need for attention was part of a child's pattern of growing up, and until the White House period, Caroline actually saw so little of her father that she felt impelled constantly to call his attention to her.

Caroline was the family's most delightful news leak to the press. It was she who alerted reporters to the fact that her daddy was "sitting upstairs with his shoes and socks off and doing nothing."

Then there was the time her father offered two television men a drink after they had been recording an interview with Eleanor Roosevelt. "They've already had a drink, Daddy," volunteered Caroline helpfully. "There's their glasses."

Jacqueline was determined to give her children privacy. Yet her experiences as an inquiring camera girl with the Eisenhower nieces should have reminded her how readily children talk.

White House Press Secretary Pierre Salinger had no easy task where the Kennedy children were concerned. Everything about them made human interest news copy. One Christmas, Jacqueline gave Salinger her photograph with this autograph: "To Pierre, from the greatest cross he has to bear."

Although she said in no uncertain terms that she would not leave her children to be brought up by Secret Service men, these stalwart gentlemen were never far distant from the Kennedy children. Even today, though they have since left the White House, they are still guarded.

President Eisenhower told Secret Service Chief E. E. Baughman, "You don't have to worry about me—but don't let anything happen to my grandchildren." The Secret Service dubbed this request "The Diaper Detail." One important aspect of the two men first assigned to guard Caroline and John-John was the fact that they were both fathers of young children.

Jacqueline had her own problems with Secret Service men, and when they began suddenly appearing from behind bushes during her private walks along Hyannis Port beach, she quipped: "You keep doing that, and you'll drive the First Lady into an asylum."

As determined a parent as ever lived in the White House, she ordered dense rhododendron bushes planted to screen Caroline from curious eyes as she romped in her sandbox or playhouse, complete with rocking chair like her father's.

Evelyn Lincoln, the President's secretary, says the children usually paid a daily visit to their father's office. But they were wonderfully well behaved and never touched anything without specific permission. The President had a graceful way of dismissing them when the press of duties was too great. He would say, "Don't you want to go out to Mrs. Lincoln's office and see her, and get a piece of candy?" The children never took a chocolate without his permission.

Since the President and his wife believed pets are a good influence for children, the Kennedy menagerie rivaled the Theodore Roosevelt White House era when young Roosevelt kept everything from dogs to kangaroo rats in their bedrooms. Caroline's smart Welsh terrier, Charlie, is still the love of her life. There was also Robin, the canary; probably the most famous White House pet was Pushinka, the Soviet gift dog who adored little girls but hated ducks.

Of ducks and drakes the White House had a-plenty, twelve arriving with the advance of the New Frontier and another, mysteriously, from a source unknown. A thousand goldfish were placed in the pool for Caroline's special amusement, but unfortunately the ducks were also partial to goldfish.

Caroline's day in the White House began with fruit juice, hot or cold cereal, and milk before she went in to see her father while he was still at breakfast.

At approximately eight-fifteen, Caroline enjoyed a daily ride with her father in the elevator from the Kennedy family's living quarters to the ground floor; then, hand in hand, they walked to his office.

While awaiting the arrival of her classmates at nine-thirty, Caroline was usually with her mother. The White House nursery school, composed of six boys and four girls, was held in the sunny solarium on the third floor. Alice Grimes and Elizabeth Boys were the teachers, and the children came from families known personally or officially to President and Mrs. Kennedy. The school was integrated during the second year with the arrival of the son of Andrew Hatcher, associate press secretary, a Negro.

Jacqueline and the other mothers took turns in looking after the class for varying periods during the first year. The children listened to stories, joined in noncompetitive games, played with blocks, and sang "Baa, Baa, Black Sheep" and "Frère Jacques." Caroline was a determined leader.

After a break for refreshments, the youngsters, while listening to more stories, rested on blankets spread over the floor. On fine days they played out of doors, and school ended at noon.

Lunch was the special meal for Caroline. She was joined by her mother and, whenever possible, by her father. Afterward came a one-to-three afternoon rest period, followed by a walk in the grounds, Caroline and her mother taking turns at pushing John in his baby carriage. After supper came Caroline's red-letter hour, at which time one of her parents read to her.

On weekends at their Virginia retreat, Glen Ora, President Kennedy liked to invent special bedtime stories for Caroline. She would sit, bundled in robe and pajamas, spellbound on his knee. The stories generally involved Charlie, the Welsh terrier, and Bruin, a big brown bear that Caroline liked to believe was hers. Her father could mimic both Charlie and Bruin most realistically and such a story would often begin:

"I heard Bruin and Charlie having a chat the other day. Bruin was saying that Charlie must have a soft time living in the White House and Glen Ora, and Charlie was quite angry with Bruin. He said, 'You don't know what you're talking about. I've got a real tough job here. I've acres of ground to patrol. I've got to keep the ducks and the squirrels at the White House in line. I've got to guard Caroline. . . .' "

Caroline is fond of telephones, and her most regular caller, when they were both three and a half, was her cousin, Stephen Smith. She is partial to picnics, boat rides and cartoon movies.

When brother John began to take an interest in the world around him, his favorite port of call was Caroline's bedroom where he was intrigued by the stuffed animals, dolls, and two bird cages. Caroline's record player pleased him most of all.

John, at one year, weighed twenty-three pounds, was thirty inches tall, and had seven teeth. He spent two hours out of doors each day and his favorite toy was the colored French rooster given him by the wife of President de Gaulle.

Upon becoming First Lady, Jacqueline Kennedy found the loss of her privacy "frightening," and she tried to preserve what privacy she could for her family. However, when the President made public appearances without her, the crowds would shout: "Where's Jackie?" To lead two lives, as First Lady and as wife and mother, was not easy; once, explaining why she did not accompany her husband more often during his official trips, she said: "The official side of my life takes me away from my children a good deal. If I were to add political duties, I would have practically no time with the children, and they are my first responsibility. My husband agrees with this. If he felt I should go on these trips, I would."

Perhaps this is why she felt so close an affinity for Mrs. Harry S Truman, and why Bess Truman is her favorite First Lady.

"She brought a daughter to the White House at a most difficult age," explained Jacqueline, "and managed to keep her from being spoiled so that she has made a happy marriage, with lovely children of her own. Mrs. Truman kept her family close together in spite of White House demands, and that is the hardest thing to do."

Although Jacqueline thought the unofficial side of the First Family's lives had been overemphasized in the news, she also said, "The press has been very interested in my official projects and has helped such things as the restoration [of the White House] immensely."

Caroline, whom her mother wished to protect from the limelight, was nevertheless allowed to witness events of historical importance which might be good for her to recall in later years. The American astronaut's visit was one such occasion; another was the first important party given by President and Mrs. Kennedy for the diplomatic corps. Caroline sat quietly watching from a seat on the staircase, and the

Marine Band played "Old MacDonald Had a Farm," specially for her.

On March 11, 1961, it was another little Kennedy who made the headlines. The New York *Herald Tribune* bannered their story: "IT'S CHILDREN'S HOUR AT THE WHITE HOUSE."

Robert F. Kennedy, Jr. (Bobby Junior), seven-year-old son of Attorney General Robert F. Kennedy, had even written his uncle for an appointment. The letter read:

> "Dear Jack:
>
> I would like to see you soon.
>
> By Jack."

On the other side of the paper was the block-lettered word: "Bobby."

He was given the appointment, arriving at the White House that noon. The official list of callers carried the name: "Master Robert F. Kennedy, Jr.," after the names of the Vice President, Secretary of State Dean Rusk, and Secretary of Defense Robert S. McNamara.

Bobby Junior was brought to the Executive Mansion by his mother, Ethel, but as the appointment was for her son, she did not go in to see the President. The youngster was neatly dressed in a gray flannel suit, short pants, blue shirt and tie. He had brought a present for his uncle, something with black and yellow spots that resembled a lizard. The day before, Bobby Junior had caught the creature in the family swimming pool at "Hickory Hill," and now the "something" was contentedly basking in a large crystal vase.

"What is it?" asked Uncle Jack.

"I don't know what it is. I caught it in the pool. They bite."

"He's turned over," said the President. "What do you want me to do with him?"

"Put him in the fish room," said Bobby.

"He's too good for the fish room," said his uncle. "We'll put him in the pool."

(The Fish Room at the White House received its name because of the tanks of tropical fish displayed there during President Franklin D. Roosevelt's administration.)

Then the President inquired: "What do you call him?"

"Shadrach," was the solemn reply.

Later President Kennedy, trying to keep a straight face, remarked to visiting newsmen: "Wasn't it nice of him to bring this present?"

Two hours earlier, Bobby's cousin, Caroline, wearing a pale blue blouse and overalls, had marched into the White House press office looking for an apple. She had a pleasant tête à tête with Vice President Johnson, who graciously crouched down to her level.

On March 16, 1961, President Kennedy's photograph appeared in the press with a plaster over his left eye; he had struck his head on the corner of a table while bending to pick up something for Caroline. Although no stitches were required, Press Secretary Salinger said the cut was "pretty deep."

Just prior to Thanksgiving that year, Caroline and her father figured in another human episode. Seated on his knee in the helicopter that would fly them to Andrews Air Force Base, near Washington, where they would board a plane for Hyannis Port, Caroline suddenly spied Pushinka, the white puppy given her by Soviet Premier Nikita Khrushchev.

Before President Kennedy could stop her she had vacated both his knee and the helicopter. Racing across the lawn, her father in hot pursuit, she dropped down beside Pushinka to give the animal a loving pat.

Caroline solemnly explained that she had forgotten to bid her pet good-by.

At the age of four, it was noted that Caroline, with red blondish hair and blue eyes, favored her father, while John Junior, at one, with dark brown hair and eyes, looked much like his mother.

Writing in the British newspaper, the *Sunday Dispatch*, David English gives us a fascinating glimpse of Jacqueline Kennedy in 1961. He said:

> There is a tremendous closeness between her and three and a half year old Caroline, which is quite delightful to watch. She encourages her daughter to do things with her, painting, walking, cycling. 'That's about the only togetherness there is in this house,' she grins.
>
> There is a great deal of significance in that remark. For Jacqueline Kennedy has tended to shy away from all things that conformist America sees as the right pattern of family life. . . .
>
> Togetherness: Always doing exactly the same things

as a family. 'Jack has some interests that are purely his and I have also.'

Club work: 'I will never be a committee woman or a club woman,' she said flatly. 'I am not a joiner.'

Conformity: She has always chosen her own hair styles and clothes, whatever the fashion of the day might have been. She stuck coolly to the bouffant hair style long after it had disappeared from current styles.

In spite of such individuality, both the young Kennedys achieved tremendous popularity during their short, bright sojourn in the White House. A simple yet eloquent example of this can be gleaned from the following letter sent to President Kennedy by Mrs. Robert F. Laas of Houston, Texas:

"Yesterday, for the first time in my life, I saw the President of the United States, in person at Rice Stadium.

"I am twenty-seven years old, a registered nurse, housewife and mother of three lovely children. My husband is a school teacher.

"I wish I could take my pride in my country and my President and feed it to my children like candy so they in their young world could taste the sweetness of such a thing as soon as possible and have them grow up in the knowledge of how truly blessed we are to live in America.

"I wept openly when I saw you yesterday. Openly and proudly because I am so proud to be an American and live in this beautiful and free country of mine.

"I think you are a very gracious visitor and that it must indeed be trying and difficult at times to have to give so freely of yourself to a whole nation. Also, it must be quite unnerving at times to realize that thousands and thousands of people hang on your every word, applaud at your every little appearance, and most of all it must be very comforting to know that most of us pray for your good health and proper judgment in all things."

Although this letter was among thirty thousand others received that week, it was brought to the President's attention. He replied:

"Dear Mrs. Laas:

How thoughtful of you to take time to write me so graciously. I do indeed admire your patriotic spirit, and thank you for your kind expressions. You may be sure the

Houston visit will be a memorable occasion for me, and I shall long remember the hospitality extended me there.

Sincerely yours,
John F. Kennedy."

During August 1963, while John, Junior stayed with his maternal grandmother, Mrs. Hugh D. Auchincloss, at Newport where his father visited him, Jacqueline was vacationing in Italy with Caroline. The Italian *paparazzi* (free-lance photographers) had a field day with so photogenic a mother-daughter team. The Kennedys stayed in the sun-drenched town of Ravello with Princess Lee Radziwill, Jacqueline's sister, who had rented a villa there. Lee's son, Anthony Radziwill, aged three, made a perfect playmate for four-year-old Caroline.

On Jacqueline's first day in the medieval town some fifty *paparazzi* were awaiting her arrival at the Conca Dei Marini Beach. They had set themselves up in a launch seventy-five yards offshore. Finally, when the U.S. Secret Service men and Italian police began to complain at their efforts to photograph the American First Lady, Jacqueline sent word that she would allow them ten minutes for photographs.

After photographing Jacqueline in a green, arabesque swim suit and Caroline sporting "pink Bikini bottoms," the *paparazzi* gallantly serenaded Jacqueline with "Anchors Aweigh" in broken English.

Caroline delighted the cameramen. When they took her picture, she retaliated with a toy camera out of which popped a clown, his tongue balancing a raspberry.

Caroline adored the local children. During the three weeks in Ravello, she gave a party for the daughters of a boatman, a laborer and a carpenter. Language seemed to be no barrier. Later Jacqueline told the Mayor of Ravello that one of the best parts of her vacation was the opportunity it gave Caroline to "play with Italian children of her age."

When the First Lady stayed out late one night to watch a group of Italians dance a tarantella in her honor she was publicly chastised by a Colorado church official for being out until the early morning hours. He also found fault with her one-piece swimsuit. However, conditioned by this time to such criticism, Jacqueline could take courage from an editorial published in the Nevada (Missouri) *Daily Mail,* the previous October 19th:

GOOD SENSE OF TIMING

Pictures of Mrs. Jacqueline Kennedy swinging a golf club in Capri pants probably do not cause the feminine mutterings that kind of thing did a year ago.

Seeing shots of her in such outfits at Cape Cod in 1960, a good many conservative American ladies shuddered at the thought of "that girl" in the White House. They had visions of her greeting the Queen of Greece in shorts.

Since then, U.S. women—not to mention their foreign sisters—have learned to know the First Lady better. They have watched her bend White House protocol to accommodate a refreshing informality, and watched her decorate her new home with devotion and good taste.

And while she may bend protocol, she doesn't break it. Furthermore, she seems to know very well when to wear a dress and when to don Capri pants.

The carefree Italians took Jacqueline Kennedy and Caroline to their hearts. They liked the way the First Lady water-skied, baby-sat, shopped, and enjoyed their noisy firework displays. Most of all, during her stay, they appreciated the message of sympathy she penned to earthquake victims in Naples, twenty miles away:

"I am deeply distressed by the destruction caused by the earthquake in Southern Italy," she wrote.

"The past two weeks have reaffirmed my admiration and affection for the people of this part of the world and filled me with gratitude for all their kindness and courtesy. That they, who give so much in heart and spirit, should suffer loss of life and home, is truly a calamity. I pray that all who have suffered may speedily be helped in their great need."

Sociologists tell us that the choice of a home is often a revealing factor in the personality of its owner. Certainly, Jacqueline's tastes are indicated in her choice of the small house in Georgetown, the rented estate in Virginia, the country home the Kennedys did not really have time to inhabit, and the series of charming rented houses that led to the White House.

The Kennedys were not partial to Camp David, the former President Eisenhower's woodland retreat. Instead they leased the elegant and secluded estate of Mrs. Raymond Tartiere in Virginia.

Glen Ora is a pale yellow stucco and stone structure

surrounded by four hundred acres of woodland. It is situated in a famous fox-hunting country. It dates back to about 1810 and to Jacqueline's delight, the furnishings are French. A map of ancient Paris was the covering for one wall in the dining room. Even the terraced gardens were laid out in the French manner.

Usually Jacqueline and the children arrived early for the weekend; the President came later, carrying his well filled alligator brief case. Although he brought work with him, he was able to get some relaxation, too.

Jacqueline rode here. She was a member of the Orange County Hunt Club, since the time her husband was in the Senate.

"What does Mrs. Kennedy's husband do?" asked a club official of her sponsor, Mrs. Paul Fout.

"He's in politics," Mrs. Fout replied.

The Glen Ora days were happy for the First Family. There were walks in the woods to play catch with Charlie, Caroline's beloved dog. There were the Sunday church services, and the papers to read and plenty of time to play with the children. Ethel and Bobby Kennedy were frequent dinner guests. The President, who loved driving in an old station wagon, got stuck twice in two weeks in the mud, and had to be rescued by the Secret Service.

One of the most enchanting mother-daughter pictures was taken of Mrs. Kennedy and Caroline as they were driving together through the Virginia countryside in their pony cart. Jacqueline as a child had enjoyed a similar mode of travel, and her versatility at simultaneously controlling the pony's reins and three-year-old Caroline was much commented upon, but then, nothing ever seemed to ruffle this First Lady.

Although all the family loved Glen Ora, Mrs. Kennedy longed for a weekend retreat truly their own. Pamela Turnure, Mrs. Kennedy's press secretary, found herself still denying stories that the Kennedys were building a Virginia hunt country retreat as "absolutely untrue," moments before Pierre Salinger confirmed the information.

The ranch house they built in Virginia, scarcely finished before John F. Kennedy's tragic death, was at first named "Atoka." Jacqueline has since changed it to "Wexford," in honor of the late President's ancestral county in Ireland.

At Hyannis Port, the various members of the Kennedy family have their own homes close to that of their parents,

Joseph and Rose. The John F. Kennedys' "Little White House," built of New England clapboard, stands next to the large, ten-bedroom senior Kennedy residence which has its own private movie theatre.

It was at the Hyannis Port dwelling, with its simple New England furnishings, that Jacqueline and Jack Kennedy awaited the results of the election that sent him to the White House.

Here they both enjoyed the beauties of the New England shore, and reports of a skin-diving First Lady soon filtered into the nation's newspapers.

A baseball diamond and football field were necessary appurtenances to what has often been called the Kennedy Compound.

After becoming First Lady, Jacqueline in an interview proceeded to dispose of a Kennedy myth. She had once been quoted as saying: "Instead of playing tennis one day and going sailing the next, like other people (her Kennedy in-laws) start right out early in the morning and go through tennis, swimming, golf, touch football and everything else they can think of. Then at night, they play parlor games. It wears me out just to watch them."

Concerning such legends she now said: "One is that the Kennedys are a crazy lot who play touch football all the time. I don't think they've played football in six years, and that was when the youngest boy was on the team at Harvard. They don't sit around playing parlor games either. They aren't together that much any more. The Kennedys are a big and happy family, and I enjoy being with them, but this 'togetherness' has been overplayed."

The "Winter White House" at Palm Beach, Florida, was a study in elegance. It was located at 601 North County Road and the street was lined with subtropical flora—jasmine, hibiscus, poinsettia and palmetto.

A white Regency-style house with marble spiral staircase, its living room had a magnificent panoramic view of the sea. Evenings the First Family were able to enjoy movies in the inner courtyard when a big screen was borrowed from a movie company, and the President particularly enjoyed the turquoise pool.

The furnishings were French and English antiques; the décor also included the now familiar rocking chair, prescribed by his doctor as a help in relieving the President's sore back. Embroidered in red on its white pillow was "The Loved One."

The French chef, three maids, two Filipino stewards, a dishwasher and two laundrymen were transported from the White House whenever the family was in residence in Florida.

The Joseph P. Kennedys lived a mile up the road on "Millionaires' Row," in a red-tiled stucco house they had bought in 1933.

It was at Palm Beach, in April 1961, that a plot to kidnap Caroline Kennedy terrified her family and the entire nation. Rumors reached the Secret Service that pro-Castro supporters were planning to take the child. Later the scheme became even more alarming when an informant disclosed that there was also a plan to assassinate the President and members of his family.

Two Cubans—a man and woman—and two of their friends were under constant surveillance.

In spite of this upset to her Easter holiday, an outwardly calm Mrs. Kennedy attended St. Edward's Roman Catholic Church with other members of the family. The Kennedy youngsters, including Caroline, took part in an Easter egg hunt.

Two years later, at Palm Beach, John F. Kennedy, Jr. (John-John), came in for criticism because of his long European haircut. "It's always been that way," explained a White House spokesman, adding that this was how John's mother preferred it to be.

Hammersmith Farm, Newport, scene of their wedding, always held a soft spot in the young Kennedy's hearts. Starting with George Washington, who in 1790 stayed at Mrs. Almy's boardinghouse, Newport had played host to eighteen Presidents. Millard Fillmore was snubbed by the footmen as well as their proud employers.

Writing in the Boston *Sunday Globe,* October 1, 1961, Frank Falacci gave the following closeup:

There are no silos on Hammersmith Farm—but the small herd of black Angus and several horses roaming its ninety-seven emerald acres by the sea qualify it as a genuine farm. Dirt farmers from New Hampshire and Vermont might take exception . . . Hammersmith is something you rarely see north of the Merrimac Valley. This is Newport in all its great tradition, the Newport you've read about and perhaps seen during a Sunday drive.

The sweeping lawns and pastureland, its rock gardens with Egyptian tiling, Italian vases, the statuary and lily ponds, all of these put Hammersmith several cuts above even gentleman farming.

There is the great main house—the stately manor which gazes out onto Narragansett Bay and toward the south looks over the 10th, 11th and 12 holes of the manicured Newport Country Club. Hammersmith is a picture page of Newport's greatest era.

When the Kennedys arrived by helicopter for a rest in the autumn of 1961, signs read: Welcome to Newport—President Kennedy. The mayor, James L. Maher, presented him with a certificate of honorary citizenship and a Newport tile bearing the city's seal.

While Jacqueline played golf, the President sat on the verandah at Hammersmith Farm attending to the presidential papers that never ceased to follow him. His back was troubling him but he did enjoy cruising on the presidential yacht, *Honey Fitz*, named for his grandfather.

Former President Dwight D. Eisenhower had established his "Summer White House" at Newport so the natives were already dubbing Hammersmith Farm, although it belonged to Jacqueline's mother and stepfather, by the same name.

Jacqueline had the last word, however, for it was at Hyannis Port that she had once declared:

"This is our home!"

Chapter Seven

"Syntax no longer is subversive at the White House," said John Steinbeck after being invited as an honored guest to President Kennedy's inaugural ceremonies.

Certainly the arts found a new patron in Jacqueline Kennedy. Musical evenings at the White House were to include such celebrities as Leopold Stokowski, cellist Pablo Casals, Leonard Bernstein, and Gian Carlo Menotti.

On August 21, 1961, President and Mrs. Kennedy sponsored a special concert for young people, on the White House lawn. The Transylvania Music Camp Orchestra, whose members' ages ranged from thirteen to eighteen, gave a concert of classical and modern music.

Jacqueline Kennedy's life-long interest in the ballet continued. When she attended New York's City Center Ballet on March 21, 1961, *The New York Times* spoke of her as a "guest star" who "never left her seat." Stephen Pelletiere in the New York *Journal American* also noted that "Jacqueline Kennedy has a woman's instinct for entrances."

She had notified the City Center far enough in advance so that George Balanchine, the company's artistic director, was able to include in the program her favorites: "Pas de Dix" from Glazounov's *Raymonda, Symphony in C,* with music by Bizet, and the *Liebeslieder Waltzes* based on Brahms's selections.

When Mrs. Kennedy arrived at 8:45 P.M., the crowd of five hundred standing behind police barricades had begun to think that she wasn't coming and there was a definite sense of relief in the applause that greeted her arrival. Hatless, wearing a gray brocade suit, she was escorted by Adlai E. Stevenson, U.S. delegate to the United Nations, and Prince and Princess Radziwill.

During intermission, Jacqueline remained in her seat, apparently oblivious to the sea of eyes and binoculars focused upon her. After the performance she went backstage to meet Balanchine, who had been a guest at a White House tea, and the dancers.

"Thank you so much. I really enjoyed it," she said. "See you again."

Her well-planned attendance was compared with the confusion that had occurred a few months previously when her husband decided at the last minute to see a show at the St. James Theatre. He nearly didn't get a seat. He came in a cab, got caught up in crosstown traffic, and finished up by walking to the theatre.

Tempted by Noel Coward's musical comedy, *Sail Away,* Jacqueline broke her Hyannis Port holiday in August 1961 to see it in Boston, accompanied by Mr. and Mrs. Paul Mellon and by Paul Kelland, a friend of the family. There were so many people trying to glimpse the First Lady that the play's author, unable to enter the lobby to meet her, waited in the inner lobby instead. "I loved the show," she told Coward afterward.

Education and culture in all their various forms received Jacqueline Kennedy's encouragement and patronage. She sent a message of congratulations to the National Council of Negro Women and backed their fund-raising drive to establish a monument to the famed Negro educator, Dr. Mary McLeod Bethune.

The aged poet, Robert Frost, who read at the Kennedy inauguration, became a close friend of the President and his wife.

On November 4, 1961, a childhood wish of Jacqueline's was fulfilled at the National Gallery of Art in Washington when she opened an exhibit of thirty-four treasures buried with Egypt's boy pharoah, Tutankhamen, about 3,300 years ago.

Said Mrs. Kennedy, "I remember as a child reading about the discovery of the tomb. This was one of the things I hoped most in the world to see some day."

Wearing a Venetian red two-piece wool suit set off by an off-black mink beret, she spent half an hour carefully examining the exhibit lent by the government of the United Arab Republic.

The items shown were only a small part of the two thousand or more found when the king's tomb was first discovered in 1922 near Luxor. They included ceremonial objects made of alabaster, gold, wood and precious stones, and a pair of striped cotton gloves that intrigued the First Lady.

Dr. Mostafa Kamel, the United Arab Republic ambassador, said that his government had allowed the exhibit to leave Egypt primarily to promote interest in the massive effort to salvage seventeen temples in a section of the Nubian Nile Valley which is to be flooded by the Aswan Dam.

As Mrs. Kennedy left the museum, Dr. Sarwat Okasha, Minister of Culture of the U.A.R., gave her a two-foot high limestone statue of a Fifth Dynasty noble. The statue, found near the Great Pyramid at Gizeh, was placed on display with the rest of the exhibit where it was slated to stay during a two-year American tour of these Egyptian treasures.

As First Lady, Jacqueline Kennedy took a keen interest in the campaign to build the National Cultural Center in Washington, now to be named for John F. Kennedy.

With other prominent Americans, Mrs. Kennedy considered it a national disgrace that there was no home in Washington for the performing arts. Even the Capitol Theatre, where visiting artists once performed, had been pulled down, and Moscow's famed Bolshoi Ballet had performed in Washington, D.C. in a converted ice rink.

Mrs. Kennedy and Mrs. Dwight D. Eisenhower became the honorary co-chairmen of the effort to raise thirty million dollars in voluntary contributions for the Center's building.

On November 29, 1962, President and Mrs. Kennedy presided over a large fund-raising event that brought in more than a million dollars for the cause. At that time, on a closed-circuit television performance, both the President and his First Lady made speeches, with former President Eisenhower and Mrs. Eisenhower also taking part.

"Art knows no national boundaries," said President Kennedy.

Danny Kaye acted as guest conductor of the National Symphony Orchestra; Marian Anderson, Van Cliburn and Pablo Casals took part in the gala program, and Leonard Bernstein was master of ceremonies.

The new cultural center, chartered by Act of Congress, is to be built near the Lincoln Memorial on the east bank of the Potomac River. International artists will be invited for guest appearances. The buildings will include a hall, with a seating capacity of 2,500, for opera, ballet and the like; a theatre to seat 1,200, and a symphony hall which will accommodate 2,000. While Congress initiated the project, it immediately received the warm support of the American public.

That this was a project close to Jacqueline Kennedy's heart was evidenced by her practical support. She painted two designs for Christmas cards as her contribution to the center. Both were original water colors. One was entitled "The Journey of the Magi" and was a picture of the Three Wise Men on their way to Bethlehem. The other, named "Glad Tidings," portrays an angel heralding the birth of Christ. Both watercolors are signed with the initials JBK.

It was the First Lady's idea to design the cards for the benefit of the National Cultural Center, and Roger L. Stevens, chairman of the Center's Board of Trustees, arranged with Joyce C. Hall, president of Hallmark, to make the cards available to the general public. Hallmark Cards contributed its net proceeds from the sale of these cards to the National Cultural Center.

As far as it is known, these cards are the first Christmas greetings ever to be designed by a member of the nation's First Family, although President Eisenhower did distribute as personal Christmas gifts, several reproductions of his paintings while he was in office.

Joyce C. Hall said, "We are very pleased to be able to publish Mrs. Kennedy's Christmas card designs and to cooperate in this fashion with the National Cultural Center.

"Mrs. Kennedy's work is in excellent taste and displays an unusual amount of craftsmanship. She has managed to express in these little water colors a great deal of her own feelings about Christmas, and, at the same time, the universal spirit of Christmas and the real significance of the day. . . ."

Not since the days of vivacious Dolley Madison has a First Lady shown such interest in saving the White House treasures as Jacqueline Kennedy did.

When the British set fire to the city of Washington on August 24, 1814, it was Dolley who made it her business to save what she could from the White House. And now having survived war, fire, and the thirty-three Presidential families who had occupied it, it was no decorator's ideal. It therefore became the dedicated task of Jacqueline Kennedy, as First Lady, to "restore" the interior of the mansion.

Her "project," as she called it, was to refurbish the White House with authentic furnishings belonging to the early 1800's when it was built. Upon moving in, she was appalled to discover that this most important house in the nation was furnished with an amazing conglomeration of art treasures, reproductions and pieces of slight artistic or historic value.

"I think the White House should show the wonderful heritage that this country has," said Mrs. Kennedy. "We had such a wonderful flowering in the late eighteenth century. And the restoration is so fascinating—every day you see a letter that has come in from the great-great-grandson of a President. It was such a surprise to come there and find so little that had association and memory. I'd feel terrible if I had lived here for four years and hadn't done anything for the house."

As wife of the President-elect, Jacqueline had been shown around the White House by Mamie Eisenhower, and been dismayed. Later, she complained to her husband: "It looks like a house where nothing has ever taken place. There is no trace of the past."

Mrs. Eisenhower had often wished to see the finest antiques placed in the White House. Mrs. Truman had tactfully suggested that Congress make an appropriation to redecorate it. This came to $213,000 for the furnishing of all the rooms, but Mrs. Kennedy's Green Room restoration alone would cost more than that.

Mrs. Calvin Coolidge had had to abandon her idea of bringing new furnishings into the Executive Mansion when her appeal to fellow Americans met with little response.

Fortunately, Jacqueline Kennedy came to the White House at a time when Americans were showing more interest in saving their national heritage, and then, too, furnishings and financial gifts for the restoration were tax deductible. Three days after her husband's inauguration, she invited David Finley, chairman of the National Commission of Fine Arts, and John Walker, Director of the National Gallery of Art, for a special White House tour. She then explained exactly what she wanted to do. The Kennedys' friend William Walton was also in the party; he later described it as "a general look-around to see what the joint is like."

"Everything in the White House must have a reason for being there," Jackie explained. "It would be sacrilege merely to 'redecorate' it, a word I hate. It must be restored, and that has nothing to do with redecoration. That is a question of scholarship."

The only record she could find of White House purchases made in past years was an incomplete catalogue prepared by the National Park Service which fortunately had been kept by James West, White House head usher.

Later, speaking of Jacqueline's zeal for bringing authentic White House furnishings "home" again, one of the committee members remarked: "When the First Lady gets on the trail of something, she never gives up. If you have a bed that used to be in the White House, she'll have you sleeping on the floor before you know what happened."

President Kennedy didn't object to his wife's plan to restore the West Wing reception room, but he made one stipulation: that she allow the stuffed fish he'd caught on their Mexican honeymoon to stay, even if it did upset her new color scheme.

It stayed.

Abraham Lincoln's famous walnut bed with the bunches of carved grapes upon each corner stood like a great oasis in a room containing no other item belonging to his particular era. Soon it seemed less isolated, for Jacqueline borrowed from the National Gallery, Lincoln's portrait by Douglas Volk.

The late Queen Mary of Britain had spent years of dedicated work bringing the state rooms of Buckingham Palace back to their former beauty by correlating historic furnishings from other royal residences and rescuing many items that her husband's grandmother, Queen Victoria, had presented to far-flung relatives. In the same way, Jacqueline vowed that "one day this much-loved house will be as great a repository of historical and beautiful objects as any other official residence in the world."

Having formed a special Fine Arts Committee for the White House, the First Lady was delighted when Henry Francis du Pont, a Republican, agreed to serve as chairman, thus giving her project a strictly bi-partisan aspect. Du Pont, son of America's best known authority on antiques, created the famed Winterthur Museum at Wilmington, Delaware.

David Finley, chairman of the National Commission of Fine Arts, became a committee member. Mrs. John Newton (Lorraine) Pearce, who by coincidence had received her museum training at Winterthur, was appointed curator. Mrs.

Pearce's monumental task was to keep track of historic and decorative treasures in the Executive Mansion where every object must be catalogued and its authenticity ascertained. Janet Felton, secretary to the Fine Arts Committee for the White House, was named her assistant, and many letters reached these ladies from persons who believed they had furnishings that might fit into the First Lady's plan.

During her husband's initial year in office, Jacqueline's appeal to private owners of famous antiques, especially antiques with definite White House associations, met with an enthusiastic response. The appeal also caused an unprecedented general interest in antique collecting, especially in pieces from Jacqueline's favorite 1812 period. Miss Catherine Bohlen of Villanova, Pennsylvania, contributed a fine gilded armchair ordered from a Parisian cabinetmaker by President James Monroe (1758-1831), and Mrs. Kennedy was particularly elated when a little tufted slipper chair, once part of Lincoln's personal bedroom furniture, was returned to the White House by a lady from Virginia. A Moravian college curator sent a 130-year-old pink English Staffordshire plate depicting "The President's House," from a drawing by H. Brown.

The young First Lady spent many exciting, if dusty and exhausting, hours searching the White House storerooms for long-lost treasures from former administrations. Exquisite gold and silver flatware, made around 1817 in France for President Monroe, was discovered forgotten at the back of a shelf.

A great Pierre-Antoine Bellange pier table, the only piece remaining from the Blue Room suite bought by the tasteful Monroe, came to light in the White House carpenter shop. Before being returned to its original place in the Blue Room, where it now stands under Washington's portrait, the 144-year-old table was regilded, then fitted with a French marble top and mirror backing to match its appearance when it was first ordered by Monroe. The table's restoration was done by the firm of Jansen of New York and Paris, as "a gift to the Fine Arts Committee for the White House."

Jacqueline Kennedy, through her press secretary, Pamela Turnure, made it known that "she wished to thank the firm publicly, hoping that their gesture would perhaps in some way set a precedent for similar contributions."

From the $500,000 that Congress had appropriated for the restoration of government property damaged in the War of 1812, James Monroe managed to refurnish the rebuilt White House to his own taste. To prevent ill-feeling on the part of native craftsmen, these furnishings ordered from Europe were installed almost secretly. Because of the burning of the Executive Mansion, he had been living in the Octagon House, Washington, at the time of his first inauguration as President.

Dolley Madison's well-loved sofa, together with some beautiful American Empire furnishings including a handsome mahogany library table attributed to Charles-Honore Lannuier, the French-born New York cabinetmaker, were presented by Secretary of the Treasury and Mrs. Douglas Dillon. A Victorian settee and two side chairs given by President and Mrs. Lincoln to friends, were donated by Mr. and Mrs. Henry Parish II of New York.

A Hepplewhite mirror complete with Washington's likeness, and a gold spread eagle that had hung in Fraunces Tavern, New York (where in 1783, Washington bade his generals farewell), was presented by Dr. Ray C. Franklin of Mount Kisco, New York. The Jean Honore Fragonard painting, "Apotheosis of Franklin," was the gift of George Wildenstein for the Blue Room. A portrait of Colonel William Drayton, statesman, by Samuel F. B. Morse, inventor of the telegraph, was acquired from the collection of Miss Eunice Chambers of Hartsville, South Carolina.

Mr. and Mrs. John L. Loeb of New York City restored Jacqueline's favorite Oval Room. Mrs. Brooke Aston, also of New York, agreed to buy some historic wallpaper panels depicting scenes of the American Revolutionary War that were found in a London antique shop.

Another important gift was a magnificent white marble mantelpiece of French design (1817-1820), believed to have originally been in the White House. It was given by Mrs. George Whitney, in memory of her mother, to the English-speaking Union, which in turn presented it to the White House.

The Arts Committee purchased a hand-carved sleigh bed from Mr. and Mrs. Mervyn E. Richards of Paxton, Massachusetts. The mahogany bed, handsomely carved with swans, had been brought into Mrs. Richards' family by a Portsmouth, New Hampshire, ancestor in 1805.

At the time of the sale, Mrs. Richards told the press: "When I read that Mrs. Jacqueline Kennedy had set up this committee to search for furniture of that period for a White

House collection, I contacted them. I was stunned when I received a letter addressed from the White House that said they would very much like to add the bed to the collection."

Mrs. Milton Black of Arlington, Virginia, gave an upholstered chair that had once stood in Lincoln's bedroom.

A portrait of President Andrew Jackson ("Old Hickory") was fished out of storage, where it had been relegated during the Eisenhower era, by the energetic Jacqueline and returned to its original spot on the south wall of the Cabinet Room. When the late Senator Estes Kefauver and Senator Albert Gore, both of Tennessee, asked President Kennedy where he had found the Ralph E. W. Earl painting, he replied with a broad grin: "Downstairs . . . I don't know where."

Even the President's desk, discovered by his wife in the basement, covered by an old piece of green baize, had most recently served as the base of a television set.

It was made from ship's timbers belonging to H.M.S. *Resolute,* a British vessel caught in the ice near Barrow Strait in 1854. The *Resolute* was one of five ships sent from England in 1854 to search for the explorer Sir John Franklin, who in 1845 had sailed from England in search of a northwest passage. In 1855, the ship was found abandoned by her crew and drifting in pack ice in Davis Strait, by Captain Buddington of the American whaling ship *George Henry*. After his crew had cut the ship free, it was sailed back to the United States, refitted by the government and then presented to Queen Victoria. Later, during the 1870's when the *Resolute* was scrapped, the British government ordered that a desk be made from some of her timbers and presented in appreciation to the American President, Rutherford B. Hayes.

Jacqueline Kennedy thought it only fitting that such a seafaring desk should be used by a President with a naval background.

The Vice President of the United States, together with the majority and minority leaders of the Senate, permitted Mrs. Kennedy to remove a fine chandelier from the Senate office of the Vice President and return it to its original White House home, where it now hangs in the Treaty Room. According to tradition, President Theodore Roosevelt, annoyed by the tinkling prisms, had sent it to the Vice President's office to keep him awake.

In two mysterious bundles, Jacqueline discovered rugs woven in 1902 for Theodore Roosevelt, whose taste she often found in sympathy with her own.

Popular "Teddy" Roosevelt was left to undo all the harm done by a predecessor, President Chester Alan Arthur (1830-1886), who in 1881 had "redecorated" the White House with little, if any, taste.

Likening his official home to a "badly kept barracks," President Arthur sold twenty-four wagonloads of its most priceless antique furnishings before calling in Louis Tiffany to replace them with the most flamboyant pieces of Victoriana.

Theodore Roosevelt employed the firm of architect, Stanford White, to supervise his renovation, noting later, "During my incumbency of the presidency, the White House . . . was restored to the beauty, dignity and simplicity of its original plan."

A bust of John Bright, British statesman who was a friend of the Union in the Civil War, was found, in company with those of Christopher Columbus and several American Presidents, by Mrs. Kennedy and Mrs. Pearce in one of the gentlemen's washrooms.

The First Lady arranged with the committee to report every Fourth of July on the previous year's progress. In the first such report, their accounting showed that American citizens had contributed furniture which once belonged to George Washington, Abraham Lincoln, James and Dolley Madison, James Monroe, Martin Van Buren, Daniel Webster, and Nellie Custis (George Washington's step-granddaughter).

A White House announcement confirmed that it was the intention of the Fine Arts Committee to search primarily for American furnishings "so that the White House could become a museum of our country's heritage, and a testimonial to American fine arts and cabinetmaking."

Jacqueline Kennedy, while still in the hospital following the birth of her son John, began to study all she could find written concerning the White House. Before the election she had told friends: "As soon as Jack ran for President, I decided that if he were elected, I would make restoring the White House my project. Presidents' wives have an obligation to contribute something."

She also remarked: "People who visit the White House see practically nothing that dates before 1900. Young people should see things that develop their sense of history." This was the beginning of the monumental task she would lovingly refer to as "my project."

Also, she wanted the rooms to look "beautiful and lived in" with pretty flowers in the vases and fires cheerfully burning in the hearths. When she moved into the Executive Mansion, smoking chimneys were a great nuisance. Since the 1948 Truman restoration, the majority of the fireplaces had never been used.

As an eleven-year-old, Jacqueline had first been taken on a tour of the White House with her mother. She recalled that it didn't make much of an impression because there wasn't even a guidebook to be had. She enjoyed far more Washington's home at Mount Vernon, the National Gallery of Art, and the F.B.I. headquarters, the latter "especially because they fingerprinted me."

Now, rummaging through the maze of rooms, she became even more conscious of the presence of American history "both of the past and present. . . ." Warming to her "project" she said, "Like every President's wife, I'm here only for a brief time. I want to do this."

She never quite forgot the little girl without the guidebook that she once had been. After proofreading and helping with the layout, she wrote the introduction to a new White House guide, which in six months sold 350,000 copies.

"This guidebook," she said, "is for all the people who visit the White House each year. May I remind you that many First Families loved this house, and that each and every one left something of themselves behind in it, as you do now by the effort you have made to come here."

Mrs. Kennedy and her helpers catalogued more than 26,500 items in the White House. Commenting on what his wife had done, President Kennedy spoke proudly of "her concentration on giving historical meaning to the White House," adding: "The restoration had been a more formidable operation than anyone realized. . . . The organization of the committees was an impressive executive job. Mrs. Kennedy displayed more executive ability for organization than I had imagined she had."

There were, of course, those who criticized Jacqueline's fondness for French furnishings. She had some comfort in knowing that those brought by President Monroe from France had been branded as "too expensive." However, William Lee, his aide, wrote in its defense at that time, "Concerning the furniture ordered from France . . . it must be acknowledged that the articles are of the very first quality . . . substantial furniture which should always remain in its place and form, as it were, a part of the house, such as could be handed down through a succession of Presidents, suited to the dignity and character of the nation."

The elegant Red Room, which caused Jacqueline not a few headaches, because of its many reproductions, was much improved through the efforts of her committee. Here stands Dolley Madison's sofa upholstered with cerise silk similar to that used on the walls. There is also a rosewood chair from Lincoln's time, and an inkstand dated 1804, that belonged to Thomas Jefferson, the third President.

Mrs. Kennedy found that the first-floor library contained more murder mysteries than any other books. These were soon replaced with books written by American Presidents, and other volumes of equal historical interest.

During 1961, over 1,300,000 people toured the White House, more than ever before.

In February, 1962, a television audience estimated at 48,000,000 watched "A Tour of the White House with Mrs. John F. Kennedy," which had been taped a month previously. Jacqueline had spent eight hours perfecting it with Charles Collingwood, the newscaster. Her lively ability to relate anecdotes about other White House occupants was reminiscent of her Inquiring Camera Girl days. Ulysses S. Grant's remodeling of the East Room, she mischievously described as being a "unique mixture of two styles, Ancient Greek and Mississippi River Boat." Both program and narrator were hailed by television critics, educationists, historians, to say nothing of her fellow Americans across the nation. The program was later repeated, the unique transcript being published in book form.

Of her restoration Mrs. Kennedy admitted: "I have worked harder on this project than I ever have on anything, and so it has been especially gratifying."

Even the White House grounds did not escape her discerning eye for she is a perfectionist. The rose garden that flanked the President's office became a formal one, more in keeping with its surroundings. Future plantings would rotate with the seasons.

With so much accomplished in two years, she could truthfully say: "Now we can relax and look for great paintings and objects of historical significance, and work on filling the library with appropriate books."

Here it might be mentioned that Jacqueline Kennedy's love for the preservation of history ("Since I am married to a historian, I have such a feeling for that") was not confined to the White House proper, but to its immediate neighborhood as well. She has been credited with being responsible for the preservation of the lovely old Federal-style structures encircling Lafayette Square opposite. She was shocked when told that they were to be torn down to make way for modern government office buildings.

She discussed the problem with David Finley; then, after talking over the matter with her husband, she called Bernard Boutin, administrator of the General Services Administration who was in charge of the plans for the new offices. Plans were quickly changed so that the modern buildings would be built behind the old ones, thus saving the quiet beauty of the park.

Another popular First Lady, the late Eleanor Roosevelt, was given a "grand tour" of her former Washington home by Jacqueline Kennedy. Regarding the new décor in the President's family quarters, Mrs. Roosevelt exclaimed in her outspoken way, "I loved it. It's light and bright and beautiful."

Her keen eyes noticed many of the familiar French furnishings that had so recently graced Jacqueline's "sweet little house" in Georgetown.

With millions of other citizens, Eleanor Roosevelt felt "thrilled and grateful" for what so young a First Lady had been instrumental in preserving for the eyes of this and future generations.

"What would Martha have said?" asked the *New York Herald Tribune* after President and Mrs. Kennedy had thrown their famous party at Mount Vernon for visiting President Ayub Khan of Pakistan. Jacqueline, having been charmed by dining in regal splendor at Versailles and Schönbrunn, hoped to achieve the same effect at George Washington's Mount Vernon. Unfortunately, she awoke to find there were many fellow Americans who did not agree with her. Somehow, Mrs. Franklin D. Roosevelt's lunch of hot dogs for the King and Queen of England on the lawns of Hyde Park seemed more characteristically American than trucking framboises-è-la-crême Chantilly, prepared by a French chef, up to Mount Vernon.

The grounds had been specially sprayed with insect

repellent before the one hundred and thirty-five special guests arrived. President Kennedy, accompanied by his First Lady, resplendent in white lace with a chartreuse sash, leisurely brought most of their guests on a flotilla of four boats from Washington to the Mount Vernon landing.

Dinner was served in a special tent pavilion with a butter-yellow bark cloth ceiling and a wood floor carpeted in green. Decorative vines camouflaged the tent wires. The beautiful gold-bordered Castleton china purchased by Mrs. Eisenhower had been brought from the White House along with President Monroe's gold service.

The entire menu was French, from crab meat mimosa to couronne-de-riz clamart (chicken with rice). After dinner President Ayub Khan and his sari-clad daughter, Begum Nasir Akhtar Aurangzeb, were entertained with the works of Debussy, Mozart, Gould and Gershwin, played by the National Symphony Orchestra.

The dinner was a tremendous success, but the First Lady found herself the center of a controversy as to who was to pay for the exotic function. Not since the time when Margaret Truman had held a slumber party with two girl friends in Lincoln's bed had a First Family entertainment been so criticized. Jacqueline, to say the least, was hurt and upset, while Pierre Salinger had his work cut out for him to convince reporters that many special items were donated "by public-spirited citizens."

According to the *New York Herald Tribune,* "among the items paid for by the government, so far as could be learned, were the cost of hauling three generators to Mount Vernon to operate the special electric wiring installed in the mansion for the party; the cost of operating the four boats that took the guests to the party and back; the fuel for a fleet of Marine Corps busses that transported twenty-two White House butlers and Marine Corps and Navy personnel to the party, and gasoline for the White House limousines that brought guests from the dock to the mansion."

Writing in the Boston *Globe,* prior to the event, Betty Beale said:

President Ayub Khan will get both the cruise down to Mount Vernon and the first state dinner at our No. 1 Shrine. That eliminates the dinner at the White House, but he should be flattered that his hostess, inspired by the dinner at Versailles in the Kennedys' honor, dreamed up the history-making event at G. W.'s home. On the other hand, the Kennedys' invitation may be hard put to match this innovation for future visitors, though right now it looks as if Mrs. Kennedy will never run out of ideas.

Mrs. Kennedy does NOT have available to her an extra income of $12,000 a year recently described in print as the "First Lady's Pin Money Fund". . .

Newspaper stories referring to this fund, supposedly set up in 1917 by Philadelphia millionaire Henry G. Freeman, Jr., have noted that no President's wife has ever taken advantage of it.

The Mount Vernon party was Mrs. Kennedy's baptism of fire. In one brief evening she had discovered that nobody can possibly please everybody.

Jacqueline Kennedy's family background has taught her how to run a large household and to prepare menus, and she knows instinctively just what a special guest is likely to appreciate.

For Lady Dorothy Macmillan, wife of the then British Prime Minister, tea was served in the Oval Room, and Lady Dorothy especially appreciated this homey touch in the Kennedy family quarters which reminded her of tea in her country house in Sussex, England. There were dainty sandwiches and pretty iced cakes, just what the British love at four in the afternoon, and, for a special treat, what could have been more appropriate than fresh strawberries and cream. President Kennedy, like a dutiful husband, made it a point to stop in for a brief chat with the ladies; then, Jacqueline took Lady Dorothy on a whirlwind tour of the historic state rooms.

Lady Dorothy might have been interested to know that informal upstairs teas were initiated at the White House by Nary Arthur McElroy, acting as hostess for her widower brother, President Chester Alan Arthur (1830-1886). At that time the President proposed to Victoria West, daughter of the British Minister to Washington, and was promptly refused. The young lady later became the wife of the future Lord Sackville of Knole House, Sevenoaks, England, and mother of the poet, biographer and novelist, V. Sackville-West.

When Finland's President Kaleva Kekkonen and Mrs. Kekkonen were escorted into the state dining room for luncheon, Jacqueline had made sure they would feel at home. The Finnish flag was honored by blue and white flowers placed on the tables; Finnish dolls given by Mrs. Kekkonen to Caroline were placed in full view, and the Marine Corps band played "Finlandia."

Mrs. Kekkonen was a guest after Jacqueline's own heart, for she also loved historic furnishings. Upon leaving the White House, Finland's First Lady was the delighted owner of a special set of books dealing with American art, literature, homes, and antiques.

One of Jacqueline Kennedy's most successful luncheons was held June 21, 1961, for Premier Hayato Ikeda and Mrs. Ikeda of Japan. On that occasion the other special luncheon guests were former President and Mrs. Eisenhower. Forgetting political differences, JFK and Ike, guided by their tactful wives, turned the occasion into something like a family party and the well-mannered Japanese were delighted.

Before the luncheon, Mrs. Kennedy took Mrs. Eisenhower on a tour of the first and second floors of the White House and Mamie commented: "It looks lovely . . . some changes have been made, but it's basically the same."

Among the alterations she did see were the two Mary Cassatt paintings, *Woman Arranging Veil* and *The Cup of Tea,* both on loan, in the Green Room.

The October, 1961, state dinner for President Abboud of the Sudan was just as successful. Included in the guest list were Henry Cabot Lodge, Mr. and Mrs. David Rockefeller, Mr. and Mrs. Marshall Field, Jr.; and this is what they ate:

Filets de sole Normande: creamed filets of sole with oysters, shrimps, mussels and smelts, served with paper-thin buttered pieces of toast.

Sell d'agneau Clamart: saddle of lamb superbly seasoned, cooked only to the pink and juicy stage, and served with vegetables.

Foie gras en gelée (in gelatin) served with green salad.

Bombe glacé Coppelia, a delicious burnt-almond pudding with coffee ice cream and macaroons.

Twenty Air Force violinists in smart white mess jackets and black trousers lined the corridor leading from the state dining room across to the East Room. When they began to play romantic waltz music, the guests were electrified.

Finally, actors from the Shakespearean Festival Theatre

at Stratford, Connecticut, performed for thirty minutes, on a crimson velvet-covered stage.

Speaking of the First Lady, one of her guests later said: "She never seems to eat. She spends her whole time turned toward the honor guest, concentrating all her attention, all her charm on the foreign visitor."

Betty Beale commented in the Boston *Globe,* October 22, 1961:

> That White House dinner should end for the time being any further question as to who is now the No. 1 hostess in Washington. Presidents' wives have always held this title in name, but Jacqueline Kennedy now holds it in fact, and there are no two ways about it.

Because of Mrs. Kennedy's interest in art, literature and the sciences, forty-nine Nobel Prize winners were guests of honor at a memorable dinner held in the White House, April 30, 1962. One great name was missing—the late literary giant, William Faulkner of Oxford, Mississippi, who had declined with the remark, "What a long way to go for dinner."

President Kennedy described the event as the "most distinguished dinner during my term of office and for many, many years . . . I think this is the most extraordinary collection of talent and human knowledge ever gathered in the White House."

The guests were distributed at tables in the Blue Room, presided over by Jacqueline Kennedy, and, in the state dining room, by her husband. China from the administration of President Benjamin Harrison, decorated with blue and gold bands and the Presidential seal, was set out on blue cloths in the Blue Room. Gold cloths were used in the state dining room to complement the Truman china with its green and gold borders.

Frederic March read from the works of three American Nobel Prize winners, including an unpublished selection from the late Ernest Hemingway, and part of former Secretary of State George C. Marshall's speech announcing the formation of the Marshall Plan to help war-ravaged Europe.

Among the guests were Hemingway's widow, Mary; Sarah Gibson Blanding, president of Vassar College; and Dr. Linus C. Pauling, Nobel Prize winner for Chemistry in 1954 who only that morning had been picketing the White House, protesting against nuclear testing.

For the glittering occasion the First Lady wore a dress of green chiffon draped over one shoulder and set off to perfection with diamond and emerald earrings.

Jacqueline will be remembered with gratitude by her successors for doing away with the tiring receiving lines at official parties and receptions that were a hand-down from the time of the second President, John Quincy Adams and his wife, Abigail. She also put ash trays back into the White House. Mamie Eisenhower had removed them during Eisenhower's era.

At the Kennedys' first White House ball given for members of Congress and their families, the young Chief Executive and his wife made social history. Guests were surprised to find themselves directed immediately to the main floor instead of having to wait in line like schoolchildren. At ten-fifteen in the evening, the President and his Lady, her white-gloved left arm linked with his right one, descended the staircase preceded by White House aides wearing military uniforms. As they walked through the red-carpeted corridor into the Blue Room they were met with the Marine Band's stirring fanfare "Hail to the Chief."

Watching from the sidelines as President and Mrs. Kennedy passed between their color guard was Mrs. Joseph P. Kennedy, the President's mother. She called the scene "an All This and Heaven Too" occasion.

Asked by another woman if the precedent-shattering idea were hers, Jacqueline said, "Yes. We figured that if there was a receiving line, it would not be over until three in the morning."

In the East Room the dance orchestra struck up the tune "Mr. Wonderful," and President Kennedy guided his wife onto the floor. Vice President Lyndon B. Johnson followed suit with his vivacious wife, Lady Bird. Later, the men switched partners and Jacqueline quipped as the speedy Vice President whisked her around, "Oh, I'm getting a much better dancer."

During a foxtrot the President invited his guests to dance, but he spent the rest of the evening chatting with all whom he could meet. Jacqueline continued to dance, and Senator George Smathers of Florida declared: "She's a wonderful dancer; she's divine."

Parties were not all for the grownups during the Kennedy administration. The children were remembered at special entertainments, such as Christmas when Jacqueline gave a party for children of the White House staff which Caroline attended. Musicals for embassy youngsters in Washington were the delight of both children and critics.

The White House food underwent considerable changes during Mrs. Kennedy's day as hostess. Said Betty Beale:

> Not only has she acquired a French chef that caused one dinner guest to remark later, "The White House has now the best French food in town. It's even better than the French Embassy"; and not only has she unregimented the guests and introduced a socially comfortable atmosphere at these formerly starched to-do's; but the other night she produced something new in musical backgrounds, and the kind of entertainment that no other local hostess could match.

Looking back, Jacqueline's guest list was as dazzling as any seen in the White House during the fabulous Dolley Madison era. With President Kennedy she entertained Emperor Haile Selassie of Ethiopia, Shah Mohammed Riza Pahlevi and the Empress Farah Diba of Iran, President de Gaulle, Chancellor Konrad Adenauer of Germany, and Prince Rainier and Princess Grace of Monaco.

One First Lady, Mrs. Calvin Coolidge (1879-1957) had served ice water to her party guests, while Mrs. Rutherford Birchard Hayes (1831-1889) was nicknamed "Lemonade Lucy" because she provided lemonade instead of liquor at White House receptions. Both she and her husband, President Hayes, were total abstainers.

In contrast, Jacqueline Kennedy's formal dinners were preceded by highballs and cocktails.

Chapter Eight

"There was a special glow of warmth for Mrs. Kennedy," remarked Prime Minister John G. Diefenbaker during the Kennedys' Canadian visit in May, 1961. And this was praise indeed from the man whose election campaign had included an anti-American platform.

The visit had come at a rather strained point in U.S.-Canadian relations, for a week previously in Washington, President Kennedy, embarrassed by the failure of the Cuban "invasion," had said, ". . . if the nations of this hemisphere should fail to meet their commitments against outside Communist penetration, then I want it clearly understood that this government will not hesitate in meeting its primary obligations, which are to the security of our own nation."

Canadian newspapers seemed to believe that Kennedy was giving himself permission to move into Canada if he ever thought that country was falling under Communist influence.

Arriving in Ottawa, President and Mrs. Kennedy were given a tremendous welcome. "Isn't she lovely!" "Is she ever a doll!" were typical comments from spectators, seeing Jacqueline for the first time.

For her husband's first official three-day visit to a foreign country Jacqueline Kennedy's nine-piece wardrobe was designed by Oleg Cassini. The White House released advance details of the outfits.

For her initial appearance and jet-plane traveling costume she chose a lightweight wool navy blue sheath dress with cap sleeves and a bateau neckline. The matching wool coat was double-breasted, with a low belt, deep patch pockets and three-quarter-length sleeves.

This was the outfit she wore for the official welcome at Uplands Airport, followed by the drive through Ottawa's crowded streets to Rideau Hall, residence of Governor General Georges Philias Vanier.

For the formal state dinner and reception given by the Governor General, she changed into a long white evening gown of heavy silk with slim skirt and sleeveless belted overblouse. Next day she wore a beige, ribbed silk ottoman two-piece dress, to lunch with Prime Minister Diefenbaker. The overblouse was sleeveless, with her favorite bateau-styled neck and the slightly flared skirt had a deep pleat on each side. Over it she wore a matching silk double-breasted ottoman coat with low pockets and three-quarter-length sleeves.

That evening with President Kennedy she entertained special Canadian guests at the American Embassy; she wore a sleeveless pink-ribbed silk organza gown complemented by a matching stole.

Her supplementary wardrobe included a pale yellow wool suit, single-breasted, with three-quarter-length sleeves and slightly flared skirt; a two-piece wool dress, again with the skirt slightly flared; and a single-breasted turquoise mohair coat, three-quarter-length sleeves and low patch pockets.

Jacqueline particularly pleased French-Canadians when she gave a television interview in French—and since she so rarely consented to television appearances, the Canadians felt doubly honored.

On May 16, looking very French with a brick-red beret perched on the back of her head, she rode in a bubble-top car to the National Gallery of Art. About nine thousand people lined the route, while another five thousand waited outside the gallery, which she toured accompanied by Ellen Fairclough, then Canada's only woman Cabinet member. After viewing a special Canadian exhibit she was presented with three books of painting and sculpture, and nothing could have pleased her more.

"Oh, I love them. Thank you so much," she exclaimed. Upon leaving she said: "I enjoyed this more than I can tell you."

The New York *Mirror,* May 18, 1961, declared that "Jacqueline Kennedy captured the Canadian capital today without firing a shot. . . . Canadian-American relations had been a bit strained lately, but Jacqueline Kennedy seemed to have revived the good neighbor policy with a smile and a wave."

After her gallery visit the First Lady witnessed a private performance of the famous musical ride given by the Royal

Canadian Mounted Police. She sat with R.C.M.P. Commissioner Clifford W. Harvison as thirty-two young Mounties wearing scarlet tunics and carrying lances guided the magnificent black horses through their intricate paces.

"Simply beautiful," said Jacqueline, always a devotee of good horsemanship—a fact that had caused Canadian officials to put the Mounties on her agenda while President Kennedy was engaged in important talks. She shook hands with Inspector J. G. C. Downey, the officer in charge of the drill, who, leaning down from his mount, asked: "How do you do, ma'am?"

When one horse appeared to be upset, Jacqueline put a gloved hand to its nose and spoke softly, soon calming the animal.

Later that day, from the Visitors' Gallery, she heard the Honorable Mark Drouin, Speaker of the Senate, tell dignitaries in the Commons chamber that her "charm, beauty, vivacity and grace of mind have captured our hearts."

He continued: "Before your election, Mr. President, many Canadians searched the civil registers to see if she was a Canadian. They found that she was not, but we all took heart from the fact that she is of French ancestry."

Only one emergency occurred during the successful three-days Canadian visit, and that was of a minor nature. When President Kennedy first retired to the royal suite in Government House he discovered that there were down-filled pillows on the bed, to which he was allergic. Fortunately a U.S. Embassy official rushed a Dacron pillow over from his own home.

Said President Kennedy at the Paris Press Club luncheon, "I am the man who accompanied Jacqueline Kennedy to Paris and I have enjoyed it."

President de Gaulle was charmed, as were his fellow countrymen, with America's First Lady. *Libération*, a Paris newspaper, published a cartoon by the artist Escaro, showing the French President asleep and dreaming of Mrs. Kennedy, while a surprised Mme. de Gaulle remonstrates: "Charles!" Jacqueline throughly enjoyed the Gallic humor and accepted the original drawing from the artist.

The former Sorbonne student was one First Lady who could speak French fluently, a circumstance that delighted the French people as it had their Canadian cousins. Everywhere she went, Jacqueline was mobbed by adoring crowds and once, nostalgically thinking of her carefree student days, she wished aloud that she could just "walk around and look at the buildings and streets and sit in the cafés."

In Paris, "Madame la Presidente" proved to be a scene-stealer and her husband loved every minute of it. Abandoning her casual hairdos to meet the spirit of the occasion, Jacqueline engaged Alexandre, known in France as the "Hair-dresser of Queens," having decided, although advised to wear clothes made in America, that this "restriction" did not include her hair.

Attending her twice a day, Alexandre arranged elaborate coiffures for the First Lady. For General de Gaulle's Elysée Palace banquet, Alexandre used as his source for the hair arrangement a fifteenth-century painting of St. Catherine by Carlo Crivelli. It was called the "Gothic-Madonna Look," to achieve which he had "dressed her cheeks" with two waves of hair and heightened the length of her head with a wiglet of coils.

For the dinner at Versailles' Hall of Mirrors, Alexandre took as his inspiration a portrait of the Duchess of Fontages, the mistress of Louis XIV. Called "Fontages 1961," Jacqueline's hair was gathered in a knot and pinned by diamond brooches.

"To pay back Paris for its welcome," she wore a Givenchy designed gown which so entranced her husband that he gasped: "Well, I'm dazzled."

President and Mrs. Kennedy were lavishly entertained by President and Mme. de Gaulle at a ballet performance in the Louis XV Theatre at Versailles. Built as an opera house for the marriage of Marie Antoinette to the future Louis XVI, the theater provided a fairy-tale setting for this historic occasion, with eighteenth-century chandeliers glittering beneath the colorfully muraled dome.

Nathalie, "Europe's leading makeup expert," was also in attendance. . . . Jacqueline bathed in the silver bathtub first installed to accommodate Queen Elizabeth II . . . and fashion-conscious Parisian women, excitedly discussing her changes of dress, also copied her lipstick, called "Tender Red." She visited Malmaison with its tragic memories of the lonely Empress Josephine after she had been put aside by Napoleon, shook hands with over a thousand people, and visited an orphanage, as well as a hospital for premature babies.

The only discordant notes during the visit were the complaints of the French that they were missing the full act of President Kennedy's personality because of translation difficulties—Jacqueline's being particularly disturbed by the halting interpretation at the City Hall reception when the elite of Paris met the Kennedys for the first time.

Reuters suggested that "part of the trouble might be Mr. Kennedy's rapid delivery and the habit he has picked up here of discarding prepared texts and making off-the-cuff remarks. . . . The result is that the interpreter has to write down what he says or try to remember it."

When the Kennedys left Paris for Vienna, John Kennedy had won de Gaulle's confidence and respect, but the First Lady had captured the Parisians' hearts.

The most heartwarming, encouraging moment during the entire tour took place on June 4, 1961, on the balcony of the Pallavicini Palace, Vienna, when Jacqueline Kennedy appeared with her Russian counterpart, Nina Khrushchev. "Jackie. . . . Nina. . . ." yelled the crowd of five thousand gathered below, while spontaneously the middle-aged Mrs. Khrushchev clasped the hand of the youthful Mrs. Kennedy, waving it along with her own.

Khrushchev himself was not oblivious to Jacqueline's charms either, for when, on the evening of June 3, visiting American and Russians met in the regal atmosphere of historic Schönbrunn Palace, an eager photographer begged, "Mr. Khrushchev, won't you shake hands with Mr. Kennedy for us?" Khrushchev quipped, jovially looking in Jacqueline's direction, "I'd like to shake her hand first."

Wearing an elegant floor-length gown of pale pink paillettes, with gloves reaching above the elbows, Mrs. Kennedy had really taken the eye of the man who has most to say behind the Iron Curtain. Viennese President Schaerf tactfully seated Mrs. Khrushchev at his right hand for dinner, while Mrs. Kennedy sat in the honored spot during the activities that followed in the music room.

During the evening Khrushchev made it his business to seek out Jacqueline for a special talk. They sat together on the sofa where, judging by their smiling expressions, they appreciated each other's sense of humor. Said Leopold Figl, President of the Austrian Parliament, who escorted Mrs. Kennedy to the dinner table: "Mrs. Kennedy thoroughly enjoyed the evening. You know what she told me? She said: 'It was too beautiful and too short. I'd love to come back to Vienna and do it all over again.' "

Although earlier she had declared her intention of keeping out of the spotlight, the festive Viennese citizens crowded around her at every available opportunity. An informal luncheon became a stampede so that extra police had to be called in.

President Kennedy's meetings with Premier Khrushchev were serious, yet informal. With Secretary of State Dean Rusk and Foreign Minister Andrei Gromyko in attendance, there were twelve and a half hours of frank discussion between the two leaders on the "cold war." At lunch on the first day Kennedy said to Khrushchev: "You know, my wife Jacqueline says that Gromyko looks so kind, so pleasant, that he must be a very nice man."

Replied Khrushchev: "You should remember, Mr. President, that some people say Gromyko looks like Nixon."

Mrs. Kennedy was moved to tears as she worshiped with the President in the Gothic magnificence of Vienna's St. Stephen's Cathedral.

The building was packed. As the Kennedys began walking up the center aisle to their places in the front row, hundreds of hands waved on either side. Mrs. Kennedy blinked and said something to the President.

She wore a blue silk suit and her cream-colored silk hat was described by one reporter as being "the shape of a salad bowl." The setting in the cathedral was medieval. Franziskus Cardinal Koenig, Archbishop of Vienna, sang the Mass. There was the famed Vienna Boys' Choir and hymn music by Mozart. For Jacqueline it was an emotional experience.

She stared, first right, and then left at the tapering candles on the altar. "Let us pray for peace," slowly intoned the Cardinal in German. "For peace between the peoples of the world." The Kennedys dropped to their knees.

At collection time President Kennedy was seen to feel in his right trouser pocket. It must have been empty, for he quickly felt in the other and brought out a bill.

At the conclusion of the historic service, the Cardinal in his brilliant, embroidered robes led a procession from the cathedral in which President and Mrs. Kennedy joined. She was crying.

A Viennese visit for horse-loving Jacqueline would not have been complete without viewing a performance of the world-famous, 221-year-old Spanish Riding School whose precision-trained white Lipizzan horses gave a special show for her, including minuets, pirouettes and waltzes.

Noted the Boston *Sunday Globe,* June 4, 1961:

For the first time since she reached Paris last Wednesday, she will do the looking instead of being looked at.

While the Lipizzans can perform just about every trick in the book, they neither shake hands nor kiss them. And for the beautiful but somewhat frail wife of President John F. Kennedy, that in itself should be a welcome change of pace.

Until tonight's dinner, an official rundown on Mrs. Kennedy's hand activities showed:

Times she's shaken hands—8,042
Times her hand's been kissed—867

It's an open secret that Mrs. Kennedy has been looking forward to her morning with the horses.

During her visit to Vienna's Augarten porcelain factory she suddenly spied models of the Lipizzans, remarking that she was seeing them on Sunday.

From the former Emperor's box Jacqueline happily watched the white horses. She hardly moved during the performance except to smile or to clap her gloved hands. She seemed mesmerized by the Lipizzans' magic.

Mrs. Khrushchev was also enjoying herself—attending a recital given by Soviet Violinist David Oistrakh and a symphony orchestra. They played the Brahms D major Concerto. Oistrakh bowed to Mrs. Khrushchev at the end of the performance and was rewarded with a smile.

American students in the Austrian capital carried signs reading: GIVE 'EM HELL JACK and JACKIE, OOH-LA-LA!

One Austrian writer summed up his countrymen's opinion of America's First Lady: "Jackie is so wonderful at bringing Europe and the United States together through the love of culture: she is so shy and modest. I think we all love her."

From behind the Iron Curtain, Poland's *Swiat* magazine, read mostly by young Poles, declared:

Jackie has entered the group of a few women in the world who, today, as in times past, set the style and tone of their epoch, create the fashions, become the arbiters of authors, composers, artists . . . This sort of woman has always existed, but never before has her influence been so far-flung or so quickly disseminated. The face and silhouette of Jackie are known to all people over the whole civilized world.

Swiat also lauded her for her "lack of racial prejudice," her independent mind, and as the friend of the neglected American intelligentsia. It also liked the "homemade, naïve realism of her paintings" which were influencing young Polish artists.

"Coo! isn't she lovely!" Londoners, especially the women, gave Jacqueline the sort of welcome usually reserved for their own royal ladies, although there were those who couldn't understand why she had not been invited to stay in Buckingham Palace. Somehow a small house in "arty" Pimlico—ironically enough the old stamping ground of her former fellow photographer Tony Armstrong-Jones—did not seem quite dignified enough for the American President and his wife. Actually the Kennedys' London visit was a family and not a state visit, although the President did have talks with the British Prime Minister.

President Kennedy was godfather to Anna Christian Radziwill, infant daugher of Mrs. Kennedy's sister Lee and her husband Prince Radziwill, now a British citizen. They stayed at the unpretentious Radziwill home, the christening duly taking place in Westminster Cathedral.

Queen Elizabeth and Prince Philip did, however, give a splendid dinner at Buckingham Palace to mark the President's visit. The conventional Queen and the unconventional Mrs. Kennedy had one great interest in common—horses—and as soon as dinner was over they found plenty to talk about, there. They also spoke about the Taj Mahal and India.

John Kennedy was the first President to dine at Buckingham Palace since the 1918 visit of Woodrow Wilson. A crowd estimated at three thousand blocked the Kennedy car on its way to Buckingham Palace, making them late, and there were screams of "Jackie . . . Jackie. . . ."

They were greeted by the Queen and Prince Philip in the Green Drawing Room, where her Majesty and Jacqueline shook hands. Then, after chatting for ten minutes, they proceeded to the Blue Room where forty-five guests, including the then Prime Minister Harold Macmillan, were waiting.

The dinner menu was as follows: a cold cream of pea soup, and filet of Dover sole cooked in white wine sauce.

The main course was saddle of lamb, accompanied by salad mimosa, with soufflé of orange liqueur as dessert.

The Queen wore a gown of larkspur silk tulle with fitted bodice and full skirt; Mrs. Kennedy a pale blue sleeveless evening dress with a boat neckline in front, V-neckline at the back, and a chignon that Alexandre had added to her hair.

After dinner, fashion designers and beauty experts had a battle royal of words as to whether the Queen of England or America's First Lady stole the Palace limelight—the two people least concerned seemed to be the ladies in question. The next morning the Queen gave her Corgi dogs their breakfast, then went about state business as usual while Mrs. Kennedy, over in that little house in Pimlico, slept until noon.

Press comments in Britain and America were interesting: Britain's *Daily Mail* spoke of the Kennedys' "astonishing" welcome although "it hadn't quite the old-friend feeling of the welcome to former President Eisenhower."

The tabloid *Daily Mirror*, with the biggest daily readership said: "World peace will not be achieved by just waiting for it to happen. It must be planned for, worked for, striven for—and traveled for."

London's *Sunday Dispatch* reporter Anne Edwards wondered if Jacqueline enjoyed all the fuss. Miss Edwards said: "She doesn't want to be a star. And she doesn't quite know what has hit her. All she wanted to do when she wasn't with her husband was to look at her favorite paintings by herself. 'Why can't they let me just put on a head-scarf and a mac and walk about Paris on my own?' she demanded," referring to the recent Parisian visit.

The New York *Mirror* in an editorial had this to say of the Kennedys' Grand Tour:

> The President may not have solved all the world's problems. In fact, it is doubtful that he has solved any. But President Kennedy and his wife, Jackie, established a new mass response to the United States and to themselves as our representatives. They brought with them youth and freshness and culture—what a European would regard as European culture. They fitted the scene perfectly.
>
> The Vienna gala even more than the Versailles dinner presented this picture of maturely cultured personalities in an atmosphere suited only for those who understand

music and the ballet and who live in a world of good manners.

Europeans have long pictured the American as a very fat fellow with a big black cigar in his mouth and a very loud voice who pronounced English very badly and other languages not at all. Also we have been pictured as materialistic money-grubbers who live without benefit of education or culture.

The Kennedys fit, of course, neither category. They have had all the advantages of education and excellent upbringing. Jackie speaks French and Italian like a native and her English is well-chosen. Even Khrushchev recognized her personal superiority and spoke to her and of her more like a courtier than a revolutionist.

An ambassadress of good will, Jacqueline Kennedy was invaluable to her country. She won many friends for the United States.

Perhaps the most exotic of her journeys was her semi-official visit to India and Pakistan in 1962. Although the trip had been announced the previous November as a project "to visit educational and research centers and view historic art objects," it was postponed three times. The White House, incidentally, announced that she herself would pay for the tour.

Upon her arrival in India, she was greeted by admiring crowds who cried, "Queen of America!" She visited the Taj Mahal, built by the Shah Jahan in memory of his wife, Mumtaz Mahal, who died on a south Indian battlefield in 1629 in the fifteenth year of her marriage, after having given birth to a fifteenth child. The formal tombs of the emperor and his wife are inlaid with quotations from the Koran, so delicately done that they give the impression of exquisite needlework.

After seeing this memorial to love at sunset and by moonlight, Jacqueline confessed to being "overwhelmed."

"I have seen pictures of the Taj Mahal, but seeing it, I am struck with a sense of its mass and symmetry," she said.

Her visit was somewhat quieter than that made by Vice President Lyndon B. Johnson, which the guides still remembered. The central dome has remarkable echo qualities, and Johnson tried out a Texas-size rebel yell with remarkable success.

In Jaipur, Jacqueline rode Bibi, the thirty-five-year-old elephant, a resplendent animal with red trappings and fringed headpiece. She held Prime Minister Nehru's arm as they observed a snake charmer at work with his basket of cobras, and appeared somewhat upset by a battle between a giant black cobra and a mongoose.

At the spot where Mahatma Gandhi was cremated she laid a bouquet of white roses; then visited a home for juvenile delinquents and a hospital. Invited to go riding, she had little difficulty in coaxing her horse over some difficult jumps; but, unfortunately for his dignity, one of the Indian officers who accompanied her, trying the same jumps, was thrown. Of her own mount Jacqueline said: "This horse jumps like a dream."

When she entered a temple and was obliged to take off her shoes, reporters were able to discover that she wore size 10 A.

When she arrived at Rawalpindi, Pakistan, crowds estimated at 100,000 were there to greet her. Whereas India gave her two tiger cubs, Pakistan presented the First Lady with a bay gelding named Sardar (Chief) and she declared, "no one will be allowed to ride him but me. . . . I only hope he won't be airsick going home."

"Great fun," was her comment on riding another elephant . . . and the beautiful Gardens of Shalimar she found "even lovelier than I'd dreamed. . . . I only wish my husband could be with me."

President Mohammed Ayub Khan gave her an astrakhan hat which she wore to advantage. A visit to the Khyber Pass on the borders of West Pakistan and Afghanistan was celebrated by a feast in her honor given by tribal chieftains, at which curry, mutton, kebab, and curds were served. There were more gifts, including two delightful sheep wearing Pakistani and American flags. She touched each of them on the forehead—the traditional Pakistani form of acceptance, then looking at the mountains' grandeur, she said: "This was what my husband wanted to see most, the Khyber Pass." Pausing to listen to the plaintive strains of a Scottish bagpipe, she added, "And me, too."

The return to Peshawar was almost like a medieval royal progress. Expensive Afghan carpets had been spread on the road at intervals for her motor caravan to pass over and welcome arches were everywhere.

On her arrival in Karachi, Bashir Ahmed, a camel driver who had been brought to the United States on a visit by Vice President Lyndon B. Johnson, was there to greet her. Mr. Johnson had sent a letter by Jacqueline for his friend, saying that he was "remembered with affection from the plain of Texas to the subways of New York." Then Mrs. Kennedy boarded the "ship of the desert" and went for a ride.

The two weeks' tour was made into a motion picture entitled *Jacqueline Kennedy's Asian Journey,* by the United States Information Agency.

Meetings with other international dignitaries during her short time as First Lady were equally successful. Wearing the customary veil of black lace, she visited the late Pope John XXIII, with whom she enjoyed a long conversation.

In Mexico with her husband, she addressed a television audience in fluent Spanish, as President Kennedy looked proudly on, and her hosts were delighted. Mexican Cabinet ministers' wives were amazed at the knowledge she displayed while visting the National Anthropological Art Museum. She pleased the inhabitants of Colombia and Venezuela by addressing them in Spanish while visiting their countries with the President—and the crowd in Caracas, Venezuela, was reported to have been the largest ever assembled to greet foreign dignitaries.

Mrs. Kennedy's several unofficial visits in Greece made her many friends in that sunny land. When President Kennedy flew back to America after the Summit Conference, Mrs. Kennedy remained with her brother-in-law and sister, Prince and Princess Radziwill, in London. Later she flew with them to Athens for a week of sight-seeing and cruising amid the Aegean Islands.

Back in America President Kennedy left for Palm Beach where, according to Press Secretary Salinger, he was to get a rest after his arduous journey to Europe.

At Athens Airport Jacqueline was greeted by Premier Constantine Caramanlis and his beautiful, dark-haired wife. A protocol officer representing King Paul and Queen Frederika presented Mrs. Kennedy with a bouquet.

The quiet gathering was in direct contrast to Jacqueline's forty-five-minute stopover in Rome, where she had to take refuge in a waiting room for the duration of her brief stay because of fifty Italian photographers who were screaming "Hey, Jackie, smile!"

Premier and Mrs. Caramanlis acted as Mrs. Kennedy's hosts, having at their disposal Greek shipping millionaire Markos Nomikos' 123-foot yacht *North Wind.* The Royal Greek

Navy dispatched a large escort as a shield whenever the yacht sailed, with America's First Lady aboard, for a leisurely cruise through the fabled islands of Greece. Nomikos described his yacht as "built in the old, comfortable style."

Arriving June 10 on Mykonos, island of 333 windmills, Jacqueline was welcomed by the mayor and a huge pelican named Peter.

"Is he wild?" she asked; then, being assured that he was quite tame, she gingerly patted his head.

The mayor presented her with a costume for Caroline—a silk-embroidered skirt, blouse, scarf, bag, and silver shoes. Jacqueline herself was gaily dressed in a pink batiste dress with shoes to match, and a red babushka, knotted under the chin.

The arrival at Mykonos was delayed by a last-minute decision to visit Delos, legendary birthplace of the god Apollo, where Jacqueline enjoyed herself water skiing in the deep blue water. On the previous night, she had delighted the entire population of 2,500 on the Isle of Hydra by leaping from her seat in a restaurant dance hall to join a dozen dancers in native costume. Violins provided the accompaniment to the Bozoukia folk dance known as the "Kalamatianes."

On June 12 Mrs. Kennedy was back in Athens to visit the Parthenon with Mrs. Caramanlis. Next day, in describing the event, *The New York Times* used the headline: MRS. KENNEDY SIDES WITH GREECE, continuing:

> Mrs. John F. Kennedy, visiting the Parthenon today, said she would like to see the Elgin Marbles returned to Greece.
>
> The Marbles, sculptures that were removed from the Parthenon by Lord Elgin, Scottish peer, at the end of the eighteenth century, are now in the British Museum. The President's wife was being shown around the Parthenon by the curator.
>
> The Elgin Marbles controversy was rekindled recently when a British Labor Member of Parliament urged Prime Minister Macmillan to return the sculptures to Greece. Mr. Macmillan said he would consider it.

On the thyme-scented island of Epidaurus she found the Greek National Theater rehearsing *Electra,* the Sophocles tragedy, in the ancient amphitheater, and the players obligingly performed part of it for her pleasure.

"I don't speak Greek but I knew *Electra* and other Greek

tragedies very well from studying them at school," Jacqueline appreciatively told them.

A pleasing incident occurred during the Athenian stay when two small boys, dressed in miniature-skirted Royal Guard uniforms, presented Jacqueline with two Greek dolls. Laughing delightedly, she knelt to greet the boys, who solemnly kissed her on both cheeks. Later she dined at the Royal Palace with the King and Queen of Greece—cementing the friendship between Queen Frederika and herself.

While in Athens, Jacqueline again went water skiing, this time with the protection of the Greek Navy, and under their eagle eye, took a spill into the water.

Naval police said they had orders not to permit any pictures to be taken of Mrs. Kennedy "in her bathing suit" which, incidentally, was blue. Two patrol boats were on guard; three small speedboats kept interested swimmers and small craft away; and two news photographers had their film confiscated.

One Athens newspaper published a cartoon lampooning the whole affair, with Jacqueline talking to the captain of the yacht while sailors were landing on Delos Island. The caption read:

> JACQUELINE: Did you say landing operation?
> CAPTAIN: No, madame. It is for your protection against the photographers when you go in swimming.
> JACQUELINE: Maybe I should wear a veil.

It was not until she read the news in Greece that Jacqueline discovered her husband was using crutches again, this time for a lumbosacral strain he had evidently suffered while spading in a Canadian tree-planting ceremony the previous May 16th. Mrs. Kennedy wanted to return at once but the President gallantly insisted that it was not necessary.

News that Jacqueline Kennedy was expecting another child was greeted with delight by many Americans. Early in 1963, she withdrew from social engagements. In view of the disasters of her previous pregnancies, it was important that she take extremely good care of herself.

However, during a visit to her Hyannis Port home, she was taken suddenly ill on August 7 and rushed to the Otis Air Force Base Hospital. Here she gave birth by Caesarean section to a son. The child was premature by five and a half weeks.

President Kennedy hurried by plane from Washington to be with his wife and to see his newborn son. But his joy was brief. Patrick Bouvier Kennedy was stricken with hyaline membrane disease, an ailment often fatal to premature babies.

It became necessary to rush Patrick to the Children's Hospital Medical Center in Boston, where he was put in a high-pressure chamber to assist his breathing, and President Kennedy stood by at the hospital while a team of specialists fought a losing battle to save his son. At 4:04 A.M. on Friday, August 9, Patrick died. He was thirty-nine hours and twelve minutes old.

"We fired all the guns there were to fire," said Dr. Leonard W. Cronkhite, Jr., general director of the Medical Center. Doctors later explained that the fatal disease left a thin membrane in the child's lungs which prevented oxygen from reaching his blood.

Richard, Cardinal Cushing, Archbishop of Boston and a personal friend of the Kennedy family, announced: "He now lives in the nursery of the children of heaven."

At 6:35 A.M., Dr. John W. Walsh the obstetrician told Mrs. Kennedy, still hospitalized at Otis, of her baby's death. She was then administered a mild sedative which helped her to sleep until the President's arrival at about nine-thirty.

Jacqueline and Jack spent more than two hours together.

On August 10, Bostonians respected the father's grief by allowing him privacy when he arrived in one of four helicopters carrying members of the family to the funeral. He landed on the baseball field at St. John's Seminary, Boston, at 9:55 A.M., his face rigid.

Limousines drove the mourners about three hundred yards to Cardinal Cushing's private chapel for the Mass of the Angels. Unlike the regular Roman Catholic funeral mass when black vestments are used, at the Mass of the Angels white vestments are worn by the officiating priest. President Kennedy led the procession down a red-carpeted aisle in the twenty-four-foot-square chapel, then knelt on a wooden kneeler near the altar.

Others present were Mrs. Kennedy's mother and stepfather, Mr. and Mrs. Hugh D. Auchincloss with their children Janet and Jamie; Mrs. Kennedy's sister, Princess Lee Radziwill; President Kennedy's brothers, Attorney General

Robert F. Kennedy and Senator Edward M. Kennedy; his brother-in-law and sister, Mrs. and Mrs. Sargent Shriver; and his sister, Mrs. Peter Lawford. With the exception of Mrs. Lawford who was in a white dress, and Mrs. Smith in a black and white check, the other women wore black.

Cardinal Spellman of New York also attended, though he did not go on to the cemetery. Boston Municipal Court Judge Francix X. Morrissey, former assistant and close friend of the President was the only mourner who was not a member of the family.

The baby's tiny casket was covered by a blanket of white flowers and white carnations adorned the altar.

Cardinal Cushing, preceded by his cross-bearer, began the service by sprinkling the casket with holy water and reciting the words: "Blessed be the name of the Lord, now and forever."

His prayers of comfort for the bereaved father and the mother still in hospital included:

"Almighty and most loving God . . . as soon as they leave this world, You give everlasting life to all little children reborn in the font of baptism, as we believe You have given it today to the soul of this little child.

"Because of my innocence, You have received me and given me a place in Your sight forever."

The Mass, lasting less than half an hour, was over. The President of the United States, his face etched with grief—for as Jacqueline Kennedy later said, "Nobody knew how much he wanted this child"—led the mourners to the waiting cortege. Slowly, through quiet streets, they drove to Holyhood Cemetery where, on a little knoll, the Kennedys have a family plot.

With a soft murmuring wind as background, Cardinal Cushing said the final prayers: "Bow down Your ear in pity to Your servants, upon whom You have laid the heavy burden of sorrow.

"Grant that they may not languish in fruitless and unavailing grief, nor sorrow as those who have no hope, but through their tears look meekly up to You, the God of all Consolation."

Then the President of the United States touched the small casket . . . and said "Good-by."

Afterward he flew immediately to his wife at Otis Air Force Base where he conveyed the theme of their little lost son's Mass of the Angels. . . . "That his birth had not been in vain, for on this day he was in the Kingdom of Heaven."

Epilogue

These words are carved on the mantel of the Presidential bedroom in the White House:

In this room Abraham Lincoln slept during his occupancy of the White House as President of the United States. March 4, 1861 —April 13, 1865.

When Jacqueline Kennedy left the White House for good on a bleak December day, another inscription had been added:

In this room lived John Fitzgerald Kennedy with his wife Jacqueline during the two years, ten months and two days he was President of the United States.

Of the monumental and shattering four days that seemed to turn the world from reality into a hideous dream, two small moments stand out as a landmark of childish sweetness and innocence. One is the image of John F. Kennedy, Jr., saluting staunchly as the caisson bearing his father's casket passed by. The other is of Caroline, kneeling at the flag-draped coffin to kiss the emblem, and seeking in an instinctive movement to embrace the essence of the father she adored.

Tragedy has been a strange and fearful specter in the shadow of the Kennedy clan brilliance. Life for them has been marked often by sudden, shocking death. Joseph Kennedy, Jr., the oldest and most promising son according to family legend, died a hero in World War II. John Fitzgerald Kennedy, the first Catholic ever to attain the Presidency, was struck down at the hands of an assassin. Edward, the youngest son, a United States Senator from Massachusetts, was seriously injured in the summer of 1964 in a plane crash.

Since old Joe Kennedy has not yet recovered from the stroke that incapacitated him, this leaves Robert Kennedy as head of the clan. It is clearly Bobby's mission to perpetuate the patriarchal drive.

In retrospect, the haze of emotional involvement keeps us from estimating the range of John Fitzgerald Kennedy's achievements as President of the United States. But one fact is certain and was growing daily more evident to the observer during the last months of the President's life: He was growing in stature. He was not only in reach of becoming a great President but also a great statesman. We were fortunate in the fast-changing ambivalence of our times to have a leader who managed to combine practical politics with the visionary's idealism. He has been ranked by men skilled in political science as a humanitarian. But before he could prove himself the equal of a Theodore Roosevelt or a Woodrow Wilson, his time was cut short. However, what all of us will remember and what, no doubt, his widow will seek to cultivate is the memory of a man whose talents and range managed to combine the total New World ideal.

An old Irish proverb suggests, "The worst insult to a dead man's memory is to lie about him."

For all of his lusty enjoyment of life, for all of his gay humorous relish of his job, John Fitzgerald Kennedy detested false honors. He would perhaps be the first to deprecate the emotional frosting that has embellished the legend even before the world has had the emotional detachment to look back objectively at his character and his achievements.

In summing up the brief Kennedy period in the White House, however, all of us will remember the elegance and the meticulous attention to the fine art of living as well as the arts themselves that pervaded the White House. But what we will perhaps best remember is that the symbol of the nation in the second half of the twentieth century was personified in a gay, worldly young couple, who brought order and beauty and dedication toward peace to the country, and from whom we learned that it is through our youth that we perpetuate ourselves and our dream.

In the drawer of her husband's bureau, Jacqueline Kennedy found two newspaper clippings. One had been written while she was in Pakistan and quoted her as saying she was sad that her husband could not be with her.

The other, an editorial from the Washington *Daily News*,

commented that Jacqueline Kennedy "has even outdone President Eisenhower as a drawing card" in India.

The heart may shrivel in agony but the conditioned reflex enables one to carry on. There were obligations to be fulfilled and they were the palliatives that made the days of early bereavement bearable.

Mrs. Kennedy was spared the business of removing all of the President's memorabilia from the office in the White House. This was supervised by his secretary and the men close to him, including the brother-in-law Sargent Shriver. The ship painting, the desk set of black alligator, a gift from General de Gaulle, the coconut shell on which JFK had carved a message for help when he and his men were stranded on an isolated island in the Pacific—all these vanished from the Oval Room even before the funeral. Even in the time of supreme tragedy, the wheels of the new government had to begin working.

Jacqueline left a bouquet of flowers and a note of welcome for Mrs. Lyndon Johnson. Then she said good-by to members of the White House staff and the telephone operators in the Executive Office Building. She studied meticulously details of the last ceremony planned by her husband. It was the presentation of the Presidential Medals of Freedom. Now one would be awarded to him posthumously.

She supervised the plans for packing and storing personal possessions. Temporarily, until they could find a Washington home of their own, she and the children moved on December 6, 1963, into the elegant red brick Georgian-style house at 3038 N Street, lent them by Under Secretary of State E. Averill and Mrs. Harriman. Before the Harrimans bought it, the house belonged to William W. Scranton, now the Republican governor of Pennsylvania.

It was a gracious house with a pleasing rear garden. It was furnished with choice antiques, many of them from the Empire period, with paintings by Van Gogh, Cézanne and Derain, and seemed ideally suited to Jacqueline's tastes. It was not far from the small lovely house she and Jack had shared during his time in the Senate. Here, abetted by loving friends, she would make a valiant effort to bypass the horror of the assassination and look back on the happy time that came before it.

Preceding the arrival of Jacqueline and the children to the Harriman house was a box labeled "John's toys" and his model boat. Then came a bicycle, two parakeets in cages with pink and blue covers, a tennis racket, a secretary desk, lamps, and a case of French wine.

Half an hour ahead of her mistress, Providencia Paredes arrived with copies of the White House guidebook. Among the family effects was the briefcase with the initials J.F.K.

Half-hidden behind a screen in the state dining room, Jacqueline had watched President Johnson distribute the Presidential Medals of Freedom. Then, as the guests were leaving, she too quietly left the White House.

John-John arrived at his new home clutching a flag, while Caroline held her mother's hand. The children were in their familiar pastel tweed coats. Mrs. Kennedy, in black, had announced her intention of observing a year's period of mourning.

The children soon adjusted to their new way of life. Early in their arrival, they spent a happy Saturday playing in Montrose Park with their cousin Sydney Lawford. They made good use of the swings, slides and parallel bars. Shannon, the black and white spaniel, frolicked with them. And John-John was enormously intrigued with the mysteries of a drinking fountain which he liberally sampled.

Jacqueline Kennedy's frequent visits to the cemetery have become legendary. Nobody knows at what hour of the day or night she is apt to come here. Late on the night of the funeral, she came to the grave, escorted by her brother-in-law Bobby Kennedy and left a sprig of lilies of the valley. The following evening, after the crowds had left, she brought Caroline with her. Each week, she sends a fresh flowerpiece.

The body of Patrick Bouvier Kennedy, and of the infant girl who died at birth were transferred on December 3, 1963, to new gravesites beside their father at Arlington.

In making the announcement on behalf of the Kennedy family, Pierre Salinger issued this statement:

"On behalf of Mrs. Kennedy, I am announcing that Patrick Bouvier Kennedy, born on August 7, 1963, died on August 9, 1963, and an infant girl, dead at birth on August 23, 1956, have joined their father, President Kennedy, in the Arlington National Cemetery.

"Patrick was buried at Brookline, Mass., and the little girl in Newport, R.I. They were brought to Washington today on the family plane, the *Caroline,* and were accompanied by Senator Edward F. Kennedy.

"The family was in Arlington for the interment at which Bishop Hannan presided."

When Mrs. Evelyn Lincoln, Kennedy's secretary to whom Mrs. Kennedy had given his United States and Presidential office flags, visited the grave, she was disturbed by the sight of the temporary white picket fence which enclosed it. She noted that the late President was never the kind of man who liked to be fenced in.

On Washington's Birthday, three months after the assassination, more than thirty thousand mourners came to pay their respects to the late President's grave.

On St. Patrick's Day, Jacqueline accompanied by Bobby Kennedy and Thomas J. Kiernan, Ireland's Ambassador, placed a sprig of shamrocks at the head of the grave. The Ambassador, using a silver trowel, planted a pot of shamrock that was one of the six planted in the shape of a cross. These were the gift of Ireland's President Eamon De Valera.

Mrs. Kennedy has asked John Carl Warnecke to design the memorial to be placed at her husband's grave.

In a will drawn in 1954, John F. Kennedy divided the bulk of his large fortune into two trust funds of equal proportions. The income of one was left to Mrs. Kennedy; of the other to be shared by his children. He also left Jacqueline $25,000 in cash, together with his personal effects.

The first Christmas without her husband was sad and lonely for Jacqueline Kennedy. It was a loneliness shared by the American people, for a pall of sadness seemed to hang over their festivities.

She and her husband had decided to make gifts of volumes containing the inaugural addresses of all the Presidents from George Washington to John Fitzgerald Kennedy. The plan was carried out, and Jacqueline, in her own hand, inscribed each book. In the volume destined for Cardinal Cushing, she wrote affectionately:

"Jack was going to give you this for Christmas. Please accept it now from me. With my devotion always, for all you were to our dear Jack and to me."

On December 18, she flew to Palm Beach with the children to stay in a house lent to them by Colonel C. Michael Paul. While Mrs. Kennedy was there, Cardinal Cushing flew down to the Joseph P. Kennedy winter home to celebrate a family mass for the late President.

Shortly before his death, President Kennedy ordered three

new pieces of jewelry for his wife from Tiffany's, where he was a good customer. She received the first piece a month after his death and there are still two more scheduled on completion to be delivered to her.

Walter Hoving, head of Tiffany's, relates an amusing story about the Kennedys. Shortly after John-John was born, Mr. Hoving heard that the President-elect was in the Fifth Avenue establishment. He presented John F. Kennedy with a tiny gold spoon for his new son. Some time later, Mr. Hoving heard from Mrs. Kennedy. Her note was apologetic; it seemed that her husband had left the spoon in his pocket.

In an article in *McCall's,* Mr. Hoving adds that she thanked Tiffany's for "starting John-John off with a gold spoon in his mouth."

The Kennedy children shopped for presents on Worth Avenue with their mother, who was wearing white summer mourning. John-John chose a model jet Boeing 707 similar to one that his father had once given him, and Caroline decided on a doll shower. She also picked a rubber doll, but seemed unhappy when she heard that the doll's special wardrobe was out of stock.

"You have plenty of clothes that will fit the doll," her mother consoled her.

"How do you know?" Caroline answered, disappointed.

It was unusually cold in Palm Beach this Christmas. The children were unable to take a promised boat ride. Luci Baines Johnson, daughter of President and Mrs. Johnson, sent John-John a fire truck, which consoled him. Princess Lee Radziwill and Bobby Kennedy chose Egyptian antiquities for Jacqueline.

Next day, Princess Lalla Aicha arrived in Palm Beach to express the condolences of her brother, King Hassan II of Morocco and to offer Jacqueline Kennedy a fairy tale pink house in Marrakech, which the President's widow accepted "with deep emotion."

"It is the least one can do to console such a brave woman," said one of the Princess' retinue.

Back in Washington, Mrs. Kennedy appeared on television on January 14, 1964, to thank the world for its overwhelming display of sympathy. Neatly dressed in black, she sat in a leather office chair placed by a cheerful fire. Her brothers-in-law, Bobby and Teddy Kennedy, sat opposite her.

"I want to take this opportunity to express my appreciation

for the hundreds of thousands of messages—nearly eighty thousand in all—which my children and I have received over the past few weeks," she said.

"The knowledge of the affection in which my husband was held by all of you has sustained me, and the warmth of these tributes is something I shall never forget. Whenever I can bear to, I read them. All his bright light gone from the world. All of you who have written to me know how much we all loved him and that he returned that love in full measure.

"It is my greatest wish that all of these letters be acknowledged. They will be, but it will take a long time to do so, but I know you will understand.

"Each and every message is to be treasured not only for my children but so that future generations will know how much our country and people in other nations thought of him. Your letters will be placed with his papers in the library to be erected in his memory along the Charles River, in Boston, Massachusetts. I hope that in years to come many of you and your children will be able to visit the Kennedy Library. It will be, we hope, not only a memorial to President Kennedy but a living center for young people and scholars from all over the world.

"May I thank you again on behalf of my children and of the President's family for the comfort your letters brought to us all.

"Thank you."

The former First Lady called personally to thank her staff for handling the flood of mail that descended on her. All letters were first opened, read and translated, wherever necessary, then sent on to volunteer groups to answer. On March 17, Mrs. Kennedy was able to report that 900,000 black-bordered letters of acknowledgment had been dispatched. The cards read: "Mrs. Kennedy is deeply appreciative of your sympathy and grateful for your thoughtfulness."

It was no doubt of great comfort for Mrs. Kennedy to learn of the many memorials that were to be erected in her husband's memory. Britain acknowledged the Kennedy ideals with plans to build a memorial to him on a one-acre site at historic Runnymede where, in the year 1215, King John had signed the Magna Carta. Queen Elizabeth II had endorsed the idea. The greater part of the memorial fund to be raised by approving Britons will be used, through a scholarship plan, for the benefit of young men and women as a token of Anglo-American friendship.

Mrs. Rose Kennedy, the late President's mother, went to Paris for ceremonies at which the Quai de Passy was renamed Avenue du President Kennedy. "Never had the disappearance of a foreign chief of state so deeply moved each Frenchman, each Parisian," Jean Auburtin, President of the Paris Municipal Council, told the crowds.

In New York, Senator Teddy Kennedy was present for the ceremonies that renamed Idlewild Airport after his brother.

However, the memorial closest to Jacqueline Kennedy's heart is the John F. Kennedy Library. By March 23, members of the Kennedy family were able to report that half of the ten million dollars needed to build and endow it had already been accumulated.

Attorney General Robert F. Kennedy has worked closely with the committee on the Kennedy Library, and he and Jacqueline are further linked in this major project.

Jacqueline Kennedy and her husband's brother had been of magnificent help to each other in an ordeal that might have destroyed lesser people.

For Bobby, life since his brother's untimely death has been a walk in the shadows. While he was grappling with the details of the state funeral, he was also thrust into the position of head of the Kennedy clan. Responsibility made such demands on him that grief was pushed within for the time being. The emotional toll came later. He went through a period of mourning commensurate with Jacqueline's, and during this time of raw anguish, they were able by some miracle to give each other the moral sustenance to carry on.

The first terrible Christmas after the President's death, his widow and his brother exchanged gifts that showed their mutual warmth and appreciation. Bobby gave Jacqueline a rare bit of Egyptian antiquity, and she gave him a volume of Irish poems Jack had particularly loved. It was Jacqueline, reportedly, who urged Bobby to carry on in government service when he seemed to have lost heart for his work.

In helping his brother's widow to channel her grief into constructive efforts, Bobby is also helping himself. Some of his liveliness has returned, too. Knowing what an ordeal the occasion of her first birthday without Jack would be for Jacqueline, Bobby arranged for a party to celebrate.

Ostensibly, it was to be a dinner for the John F. Kennedy Memorial Library and the guests were to be people closely allied with the project. This was Mrs. Kennedy's understanding when she was ushered into a private dining room at New York's gourmet Four Seasons Restaurant. But Bobby had arranged beforehand with Stuart Levin, the director of the restaurant, for the birthday cake and the presentation of the birthday gifts. For this dinner, the last week of July, 1964, Mr. Levin served the shrimp in the famous Four Seasons sauce that the restaurant is justly famous for, and a simple butter cream cake with filmy roses. Mr. Levin's gratification of the event, however, was touched with sorrow. For it was in this room at the Four Seasons that the late Jack Kennedy had celebrated his first birthday as President of the United States.

Mr. Levin, who has served the most beautiful women in the world at the Four Seasons, is lyrical about Mrs. Kennedy. He stressed not only her charm and beauty but the direct, childlike simplicity that is one of her most engaging traits.

The qualities which attracted the sophisticated Jack Kennedy to the young Jacqueline Bouvier have deepened and matured. She shares with Bobby the sense of courage that is helping to restore them to a useful world. Recently, Bobby wrote in a new foreword to his brother's book, *Profiles in Courage:*

"Courage is the virtue that President Kennedy most admired. He sought out those people who had demonstrated in some way, whether it was on a battlefield, or a baseball diamond, in a speech or fighting for some cause, that they had courage, that they would stand up, that they could be counted on. . . .

"[He] would be forty-seven in May of 1964. At least one half of the days he spent on this earth were days of intense physical pain. He had diphtheria when he was very young and serious back trouble when he was older. But during all this time, I never heard him complain. I never heard him say anything that would indicate that he felt that God had dealt with him unjustly. . . . He didn't complain about his problem, so why should I complain about mine—this is how one always felt. . . ."

"We must go on," Bobby Kennedy said. He became parent by proxy to his brother's orphaned children, making them part of his energetic, gregarious brood. Jacqueline brings Caroline and John-John to Hickory Hill almost daily. While she is there, frolicking in the pool with her uncle and her cousins, Caroline grows gay and bright, and the sober young face with its shadow of premature sorrow grows alive and happy again. Caroline shows her Uncle Bobby her drawings; she clings to him as once she clung to her father. John-John wrestles delightedly with him. John, says Bobby with deep affection, is something of a rogue, mischievous and outgiving. It is Caroline who is developing a tendency to withdraw, and Bobby, sensitive to her anguish, is particularly gentle with her.

For Jacqueline, there are memories everywhere of her husband. The avalanche of books about his style, his flair, his growing stature. There are the Kennedy memorial albums, which include *John F. Kennedy—The Presidential Years*. There is a two-disc album of the Solemn Pontifical Requiem Mass celebrated by Richard Cardinal Cushing for John Fitzgerald Kennedy on January 19, 1964, in Boston's Cathedral of the Holy Cross. And there are her children.

How do you tell children, too young to comprehend, that their adored father is dead; that never again will they see his flashing smile or hear his affectionate voice or feel the reassuring touch of his hand? The thought of the children had been the concern of Pope Paul VI, when he asked, after the assassination, "Do the children know?"

Where her children are concerned, one gets a deeper insight into the healing balm of Jacqueline Kennedy's faith. Through her husband and his family, she had embraced Catholicism in its deepest and most spiritual terms, and although she insists on privacy in her religious observance, her faith is an integral part of her life.

"Let no one tell you she is not a religious person," Richard Cardinal Cushing said, "just because she says nothing in public. I have correspondence from her which shows that she feels. . . ."

Caroline is old enough to recall the days when her father accompanied her and her mother to worship. Sometimes, her mother reads to them the words that her father wrote about the uncle she never knew—Uncle Joe, who died in World War II.

"And through it all," the late President wrote of his older brother, "he had a deep and abiding Faith—he was never far from God—and so I cannot help but feel that 'Death to him was less a setting forth than a returning.' "

The children no doubt remember that their father often heard their bedtime prayers. Their mother has shown them the plaque their father kept in his office. "O God, Thy sea is so great and my boat is so small."

Jacqueline showed inherent wisdom when she allowed her children to share in the ritual of the funeral services for their father. Psychologists believe it is wise to tell children that their father is in heaven and under the care of God. So that Caroline and John are able to believe what their mother has told them. Small as they are, they have been exposed to rich spiritual indoctrination, which is without doubt a great source of comfort to their small empty hearts.

At the gravesite, before the body of the young President was committed to the earth, Cardinal Cushing said, " 'I am the resurrection and the life; he who believes in Me, though he is dead, will live on; and whoever has life, and has faith in Me, to all eternity cannot die.' "

The children were not present at that moment. But perhaps they will remember and be consoled by the memory of the Cardinal blessing their father's coffin at the low Requiem Mass at St. Matthew's Cathedral and intoning in his harsh, heartbroken voice, "May the angels, dear Jack, lead you into Paradise. May the martyrs receive you at your coming. May the spirit of God embrace you, and mayest thou, with all those who make the supreme sacrifice of dying for others, receive eternal rest and peace. Amen."

And surely they will always remember their mother's simple prayer: *Dear God, Take care of thy servant, John Fitzgerald Kennedy.*

Washington had too many memories, and time did not entirely heal. Jacqueline Kennedy took her children to Hyannis Port for the summer of 1964 and then, before it was over, to her mother's summer home in Newport. The simple outdoor life has done much to bolster Mrs. Kennedy's health. She is in better spirits and evidently has a more positive attitude about the future. She has put her Georgetown house, so recently bought and furnished, on the market. She is also disposing of Wexford, her Middleburg, Virginia, estate. It may seem odd that a search for privacy should take her to New York City, yet her chances of a reasonably private life are enhanced in the metropolis. Here there will be no busses to advertise Mrs. Kennedy's home on sightseeing tours. She has bought a fifteen-room apartment on upper Fifth Avenue, not far from the Metropolitan Museum of Art.

Nearby are the apartments of two Kennedy sisters and their

husbands, the Stephen Smiths and the Peter Lawfords; and Jacqueline's sister Lee is in the neighborhood, too. The comfort of family and friends will insure the promise of a private life for the young woman who in the last years has known no privacy at all. Her dreams are now for her children and for the memorial to her husband, whose soul has escaped from the night of our life into the peace of infinity.

There must be moments when she thinks of Elizabeth Barrett Browning, another woman who loved without self, and expressed it so exquisitely.

> How do I love thee? Let me count the ways.
> I love thee to the depth and breadth and height
> My soul can reach . . .
> . . . I love thee with the breath,
> Smiles, tears, of all my life!—and, if God choose,
> I shall but love thee better after death

Postscript

It began again for her with the release of the testimony of witnesses before the Warren Commission; information that was given to the world Monday, November 23rd, 1964. Again the memory became a living wound.

Now the world read the text of her own testimony shortly after the assassination:

"And just as I turned and looked at him, I could see a piece of his skull and I remember it was flesh colored. I remember thinking he just looked as if he had a slight headache . . . and then, he sort of did this, put his hand to his forehead, and fell into my lap."

In re-living that awful moment, she found herself the victim of an excruciating sense of guilt.

Although she had read that the shot that killed her husband also gravely wounded Governor Connally, she added, "But I used to think if I had only been looking to the right, I might have seen the first shot hit him, then I could have pulled him down, and then the second shot would not have hit him."

The sense of twenty-twenty hindsight plagues us all after a tragedy. Had the President not worn his back brace, he might have collapsed after the first shot and have been spared the fatal bullet. But the brace held him upright. Another few seconds and the limousine would have been out of the sniper's range—

The might-have-beens are the cross for the living to bear.

Mrs. Kennedy had recently made the first tentative steps toward her own emotional rehabilitation. She had planned to attend the benefit showing of the film, *My Fair Lady;* she was also to have attended a dinner to raise funds for the Cedars of Lebanon-Mount Sinai in Los Angeles. However, she appeared at neither affair. The drain on her emotions was too much. The first anniversary of the assassination found her in seclusion.

Of her relatives, her sister Lee Radziwill and her brother-in-law, Bobby Kennedy evidently exercise the deepest influence on her. And she spends a good deal of time with her children.

She has recently leased a weekend house in Glen Cove on Long Island Sound, and it was there that Caroline celebrated her seventh birthday on November 27, 1964. Just a few days earlier, young John had marked his fourth. Caroline appears to be coming out of the moody indrawn state that had worried those around her. The most recent photographs of the little girl indicate a more relaxed and happy frame of mind.

The calendar, nevertheless, has not yet offered full balm to the bereaved. Time is not measured by a sundial, and for those in the cowl of grief, it is too often still the black of an endless night.

Who can forget that this was a man of many attributes—strength and realistic thinking; imagination and a romantic sensitivity; visions that outstripped even his dreams. He made us all conscious of the values in the pursuit of excellence. A bullet shattered his potential; now the world will never know how his reasoning and dedication to peace might have changed the course of our destiny.

To love a man of this calibre and to lose him—surely this blow is enough to shatter the strongest heart. To love a man who is the leader of his country and the symbol of peace to a strife-torn world compounds the tragedy.

His widow said sorrowfully that she had never dared to hope they would grow old together.

What is there for her in the future?

Living in New York City now, she plays with her children; she works on plans for the Kennedy library; she attends small dinners with old friends. Newcomers find it rather a strain being with Mrs. Kennedy; as one said, it was like trying to make small talk with a heroic statue. She clings to her sister, Lee Radziwill and Bobby Kennedy; they insulate her lovingly against the world.

Jacqueline's image as a lovely ornament has been transformed by tragedy. She is now the Widow of the Martyred President. The public that bestowed this image upon her will not allow it to be marred. She is destined to remain imprisoned within her legend. If she shows a human side to her character, criticism instantly makes itself heard. In bestowing admiration and reverence upon her, we have condemned her to eternal solitude. We must not expect her to spend the rest of her life, a wraith in black, wandering to a lonely tryst in Arlington Cemetery.

The future holds what she chooses to make of it.

Those who revere her must allow it.